Vintage Legacies

Wrap Up in 14 Ageless Quilts
for Reproduction Fabrics

CAROL HOPKINS

Vintage Legacies: Wrap Up in 14 Ageless Quilts for
Reproduction Fabrics
© 2018 by Carol Hopkins

Martingale®
19021 120th Ave. NE, Ste. 102
Bothell, WA 98011-9511 USA
ShopMartingale.com

Printed in China
23 22 21 20 19 18   8 7 6 5 4 3 2 1

Library of Congress Cataloging-in-Publication Data

Names: Hopkins, Carol J., author.

Title: Vintage legacies : wrap up in 14 ageless quilts for
       reproduction fabrics / Carol Hopkins.

Description: Bothell, WA : Martingale, [2018]

Identifiers: LCCN 2018031424 | ISBN 9781604689785

Subjects: LCSH: Quilting--Patterns. | Quilts. | Patchwork--Patterns.

Classification: LCC TT835 .H55678 2018 | DDC 746.46/041--dc23

LC record available at https://lccn.loc.gov/2018031424

MISSION STATEMENT

We empower makers who use fabric and yarn
to make life more enjoyable.

CREDITS

**PUBLISHER AND
CHIEF VISIONARY OFFICER**
Jennifer Erbe Keltner

CONTENT DIRECTOR
Karen Costello Soltys

MANAGING EDITOR
Tina Cook

ACQUISITIONS EDITOR
Karen M. Burns

TECHNICAL EDITOR
Ellen Pahl

COPY EDITOR
Marcy Heffernan

DESIGN MANAGER
Adrienne Smitke

PRODUCTION MANAGER
Regina Girard

**COVER AND
BOOK DESIGNER**
Kathy Kotomaimoce

PHOTOGRAPHERS
Brent Kane
Adam Albright

ILLUSTRATOR
Sandy Loi

SPECIAL THANKS
*Photography for this book was taken at
Carol Hansen's Garden Barn in Indianola, Iowa.*

DEDICATION

To my beautiful children, Timothy, Emily, and Michael

CONTENTS

INTRODUCTION

As each of the four books in my "Civil War Legacies" series was published, inevitably someone would ask, "Why do you focus on small quilts—why not larger ones?" After joking that my attention span averages about 10 blocks before I'm ready to move on to a new project, I'd acknowledge that I do make larger quilts—I just haven't included them in a book. With a nod and a smile, I'd agree that maybe someday I would write a book focusing on quilts large enough to actually sleep under. Thus, with encouragement from many wonderful quilters who have purchased my previous books, I offer *Vintage Legacies*, a collection of 14 of my favorite large quilts, including a few that I've never shared publicly.

As you read the vignettes accompanying each pattern, you'll learn that several of the quilts are the result of block exchanges with a treasured group of friends. Others are inspired by photographs and purchases of antique quilts. While all of the patterns contain traditional blocks, I'm hoping that you'll be inspired to try color combinations or block layouts that might be new to you, such as those in the medallion quilts. Most of all, I hope you'll find just the right pattern for making a quilt that's big enough to snuggle under.

~ *Carol*

Enduring Love

Letters and diary entries written during the Civil War reflect the enduring love between the fathers, husbands, brothers, and friends who left the comfort of their homes, and the women and children who anxiously awaited their return.

FINISHED QUILT: 75½" × 75½"

Materials

Yardage is based on 42"-wide fabric. Fat quarters measure 18" x 21".

2⅛ yards of tan-and-cream (referred to as "tan") print for medallion center and Star blocks

12 fat quarters of assorted blue, red, green, brown, gold, and pink prints (collectively referred to as "dark"), for Star blocks, appliqué, and Square-in-a-Square blocks

1 fat quarter of brown print for branch appliqués

1¼ yards of brown serpentine stripe for borders 1 and 3

⅜ yard of cream-and-blue print for border 2

⅞ yard of cream-and-red print for Square-in-a-Square blocks

1 yard of green print for border 5 and binding

½ yard of brown-and-taupe print for border 7

2⅓ yards of large floral print for border 8

4⅝ yards of fabric for backing*

82" × 82" piece of batting

*If your fabric is not at least 41" wide after removing selvages, you'll need 6⅞ yards.

To Add Interest

To create a soft, romantic-looking quilt, select a light background floral print for the outer border, and then choose light and medium prints that blend with it. Avoid using dark prints since they tend to draw your eye to them and disrupt the flow of the medallion design.

Cutting

All measurements include ¼"-wide seam allowances.

From the tan print, cut:

1 strip, 14" × 42"; crosscut into:
    1 square, 14" × 14"
    4 squares, 6½" × 6½"

2 strips, 2½" × 42"; crosscut into 12 rectangles, 2½" × 4½"

21 strips, 2" × 42"; crosscut into:
    144 rectangles, 2" × 3½"
    144 squares, 2" × 2"

5 strips, 1½" × 42"; crosscut into:
    48 rectangles, 1½" × 2½"
    48 squares, 1½" × 1½"

From *each* of the dark print fat quarters, cut:

1 strip, 1½" × 21"; crosscut into 8 squares, 1½" × 1½" (96 total)

1 strip, 2½" × 21"; crosscut into:
    1 square, 2½" × 2½" (12 total)
    4 squares, 2" × 2" (48 total)

2 strips, 2" × 21"; crosscut into 20 squares, 2" × 2" (240 total)

1 strip, 3½" × 21"; crosscut into 3 squares, 3½" × 3½" (36 total)

1 strip, 4½" × 21"; crosscut into 4 squares, 4½" × 4½"
    (48 total, 8 are extra)

From the *lengthwise* grain of the brown serpentine stripe, cut:

4 strips, 2½" × 32" (for mitered corners)

4 strips, 2½" × 40" (for mitered corners)
    OR

2 strips, 2½" × 24½" (for butted corners)

2 strips, 2½" × 28½" (for butted corners)

2 strips, 2½" × 32½" (for butted corners)

2 strips, 2½" × 36½" (for butted corners)

Continued on page 9

Enduring Love, pieced by Carol Hopkins and quilted by Lisa Ramsey

Continued from page 7

From the cream-and-blue print, cut:

2 strips, 2½" × 28½"

2 strips, 2½" × 32½"

From the cream-and-red print, cut:

10 strips, 2½" × 42"; crosscut into 160 squares, 2½" × 2½"

From the green print, cut:

5 strips, 2½" × 42"

8 strips, 2" × 42" (for binding)

From the brown-and-taupe print, cut:

7 strips, 2" × 42"

From the *lengthwise* grain of the large floral print, cut:

2 strips, 6½" × 63½"

2 strips, 6½" × 75½"

Appliquéing the Center Block

1 Prepare the branches for appliqué by cutting bias strips from the brown print fat quarter. Cut one bias strip, 1" × 15", for the center branch. Cut one strip, ⅞" × 4¼", and one strip, ⅞" × 7¾", for the side branches. This allows a ¼" turn-under allowance on all sides.

2 Prepare the birds and leaves for appliqué using the patterns on page 13. Arrange all the appliqué pieces in the center of the tan 14" square as shown. Trim the branches to the desired lengths. Use your preferred appliqué method to sew the pieces to the square. Trim the block to measure 12½" square.

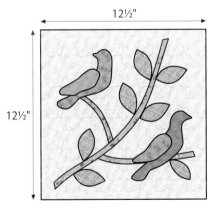

Appliqué placement diagram

Assembling the Medallion Center

Be sure to check the measurements of your blocks and quilt after completing each step, and make any necessary adjustments before proceeding to the next step to ensure that all borders will fit. Press all seam allowances as indicated by the arrows.

1 Make a small flying-geese unit with two matching dark 1½" squares and one tan 1½" × 2½" rectangle as shown. Make four matching units measuring 1½" × 2½", including seam allowances.

Make 4 units,
1½" × 2½".

2 Arrange four tan 1½" squares, four small flying-geese units, and a contrasting dark 2½" square as shown. Sew the pieces into rows, and then join the rows to make a Star block measuring 4½" square, including seam allowances. Make 12 Star blocks.

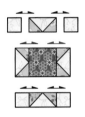

Make 12 blocks,
4½" × 4½".

3 Sew a tan 2½" × 4½" rectangle to each of the Star blocks to make a unit measuring 4½" × 6½". Join three units as shown to make a larger unit measuring 6½" × 12½", including seam allowances. Make four units.

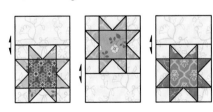

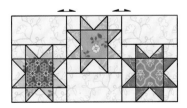

Make 4 units,
6½" × 12½".

4 Arrange the units from step 3, four tan 6½" squares, and the appliqué block as shown. Sew the pieces into rows, and then join the rows to make a medallion center measuring 24½" square, including seam allowances.

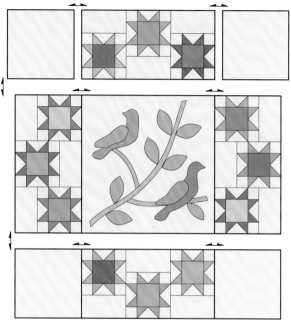

Medallion center assembly

Adding Borders 1–3

1 For border 1 with mitered corners, center and then sew a brown serpentine 2½" × 32" strip to each side of the center medallion, stopping ¼" from each corner of the quilt top. Use your preferred method to miter the corners to make a quilt center measuring 28½" square, including seam allowances.

Note: For butted corners, join 2½" × 24½" strips to opposite sides of the center medallion. Sew 2½" × 28½" strips to the top and bottom of the quilt. The quilt center should measure 28½" square, including seam allowances.

2 For border 2, sew the cream-and-blue 2½" × 28½" strips to opposite sides of the quilt center. Sew 2½" × 32½" strips to the top and bottom of the quilt center. The quilt center should measure 32½" square, including seam allowances.

3 For border 3 with mitered corners, center and then sew a brown serpentine 2½" × 40" strip to each side of the quilt, stopping ¼" from each corner of the quilt top. Use your preferred method to miter the corners as before to make a unit measuring 36½" square, including seam allowances.

Note: For butted corners, sew 2½" × 32½" strips to opposite sides of the quilt. Sew 2½" × 36½" strips to the top and bottom of the quilt, which should measure 36½" square, including seam allowances.

Adding Borders 4 and 5

1 Place a cream-and-red 2½" square on one corner of a dark 4½" square, right sides together. Sew diagonally from corner to corner of the light square. (Draw a diagonal line first if you're not comfortable stitching across an unmarked square.) Fold the resulting light triangle toward the outer corner and press in place; trim the seam allowances to ¼" if desired. Sew cream-and-red 2½" squares on the three remaining corners of the dark square, pressing after adding each piece to make a Square-in-a-Square block measuring 4½" square, including seam allowances. Make 40 blocks.

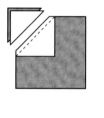
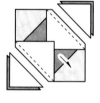

Make 40 blocks,
4½" × 4½".

2 For border 4, sew nine Square-in-a Square blocks together to make a border strip. Make two strips and sew these to the sides of the quilt. Sew 11 Square-in-a-Square blocks together to make a strip. Make two strips and sew them to the top and bottom of the quilt, which should measure 44½" square, including seam allowances.

Border 4
Make 2 side borders,
4½" × 36½".

Border 4
Make 2 top/bottom borders,
4½" × 44½".

3 For border 5, join five green 2½"-wide strips, end to end. Cut two strips, 2½" × 44½", and sew them to the sides of the quilt. Cut two strips, 2½" × 48½", and sew them to the top and bottom of the quilt, which should measure 48½" square, including seam allowances.

Adding Borders 6–8

1 Repeat steps 1 and 2 of "Assembling the Medallion Center" on page 9 to make a large Star block. Make four flying-geese units from dark 2" squares and tan 2" × 3½" rectangles.

Make 4 units,
2" × 3½".

2 Arrange and sew the units together with four tan 2" squares and a contrasting dark 3½" square to make a large Star block measuring 6½" square, including seam allowances. Make 36 large Star blocks.

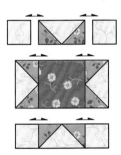 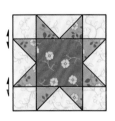

Make 36 blocks,
6½" × 6½".

3 For border 6, sew together eight large Star blocks to make a border strip. Make two strips and sew these to the sides of the quilt. Sew together 10 large Star blocks to make a border strip. Make two strips and sew them to

the top and bottom of the quilt, which should measure 60½" square, including seam allowances.

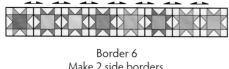

Border 6
Make 2 side borders,
6½" × 48½".

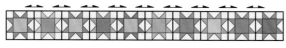

Border 6
Make 2 top/bottom borders,
4½" × 60½".

4 For border 7, join seven brown-and-taupe 2" × 42" strips end to end. Cut two strips, 2" × 60½", and sew them to the sides of the quilt. Cut two strips, 2" × 63½", and sew them to the top and bottom of the quilt, which should measure 63½" square, including seam allowances.

5 For border 8, sew the large floral print 6½" × 63½" strips to the sides of the quilt. Sew the large floral 6½" × 75½" strips to the top and bottom of the quilt to make the quilt top measuring 75½" square.

Finishing

For help with any of the finishing steps, you'll find free information at ShopMartingale.com/HowtoQuilt.

1 Layer the quilt top, batting, and backing. Baste the layers together and hand or machine quilt. The quilt shown is machine quilted with swirls, flowers, leaves, and vines in the blocks and inside borders, and a feather design in the outer border.

2 Trim the excess batting and backing fabric. Use the green 2"-wide strips to bind the quilt. Add a hanging sleeve, if desired, and a label.

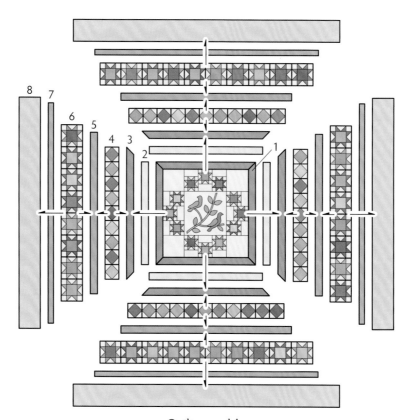

Quilt assembly

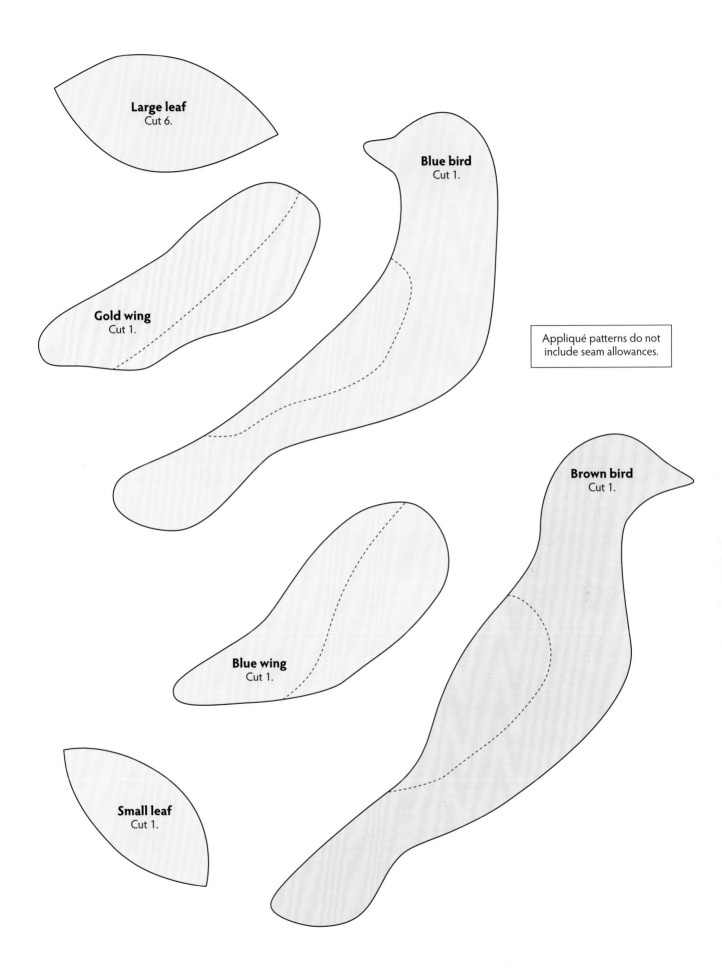

Large leaf
Cut 6.

Blue bird
Cut 1.

Gold wing
Cut 1.

Appliqué patterns do not include seam allowances.

Brown bird
Cut 1.

Blue wing
Cut 1.

Small leaf
Cut 1.

Work Shirts

A ll of the fabrics used in the Weathervane blocks of this quilt are stripes, plaids, checks, or dots reminiscent of those used in men's work shirts for centuries. According to C&C Sutlery, a clothing supplier for Civil War reenactors, the only fitted parts of work shirts were the neck and cuffs into which the shirt sleeves were gathered. The three-inch-long cuffs extended to the man's knuckles so that they could be seen while wearing a jacket, and were folded back for work. Interestingly, work shirts of the era were regarded as underwear to be worn under vests or jackets and were not to be exposed in public.

FINISHED QUILT: 73" × 93½" ✦ **FINISHED BLOCK: 6" × 6"**

Materials

Yardage is based on 42"-wide fabric.

83 assorted light scraps, at least 7" × 8" *each,* for block backgrounds

83 assorted medium or dark scraps (collectively referred to as "dark #1"), at least 5" × 5" *each,* for blocks*

83 assorted medium or dark scraps (collectively referred to as "dark #2"), at least 6" × 8" *each,* for blocks

1¾ yards of brown stripe for sashing

⅓ yard of cheddar print for cornerstones

1 yard of blue-and-brown check for setting triangles

2½ yards of dark brown check for border

⅝ yard of brown-and-tan print for binding

5¾ yards of fabric for backing

81" × 102" piece of batting

You can use charm squares if you cut carefully. The entire 5" square is needed.

To Add Interest

Reverse the position of light and dark fabrics in some of the blocks. Choose tone-on-tone checks and stripes for the sashing, setting triangles, and border fabrics so that they frame the blocks but do not detract from them.

Cutting

All measurements include ¼"-wide seam allowances.

From *each* of the light scraps, cut:
12 squares, 1½" × 1½" (996 total)
4 squares, 1⅞" × 1⅞"; cut in half diagonally to yield 8 triangles (664 total)

From *each* of the dark #1 scraps, cut:
4 squares, 2½" × 2½" (332 total)

From *each* of the dark #2 scraps, cut:
4 squares, 1½" × 1½" (332 total)
1 square, 2½" × 2½" (83 total)
4 squares, 1⅞" × 1⅞"; cut in half diagonally to yield 8 triangles (664 total)

From the brown stripe, cut:
32 strips, 1¾" × 42"; crosscut into 192 strips, 1¾" × 6½"

From the cheddar print, cut:
5 strips, 1¾" × 42"; crosscut into 110 squares, 1¾" × 1¾"

From the blue-and-brown check, cut:
2 strips, 11½" × 42"; crosscut into 6 squares, 11½" × 11½". Cut into quarters diagonally to yield 24 side triangles.
2 squares, 7" × 7"; cut in half diagonally to yield 4 corner triangles

From the *lengthwise* grain of the dark brown check, cut:
4 strips, 6" × 86"

From the brown-and-tan print, cut:
9 strips, 2" × 42"

15

*Work Shirts, pieced by **Carol Hopkins** and quilted by **Lisa Ramsey***

Making the Blocks

Each block contains a light print for the background, a dark print #1 for the squares with folded corners, and a dark print #2 for the center and weathervane corners (block corners). Instructions are for making one block at a time. Press the seam allowances as indicated by the arrows.

1 Draw a diagonal line from corner to corner on the wrong side of eight matching light 1½" squares. Sew two squares to adjacent corners of a 2½" dark #1 square as shown. Press the light squares toward the corners and trim the seam allowances to ¼" if desired. Make four units measuring 2½" square, including seam allowances.

Make 4 units,
2½" × 2½".

2 Sew light and dark #2 triangles together in pairs to make eight matching half-square-triangle units measuring 1½" square, including seam allowances.

Make 8 units,
1½" × 1½".

3 Arrange a light 1½" square, a 1½" square of dark #2, and two half-square-triangle units as shown. Sew the units together into rows, and then join the rows together. Repeat to make four matching units measuring 2½" square, including seam allowances.

Make 4 units,
2½" × 2½".

4 Arrange the units from steps 1 and 3 and a 2½" dark #2 square as shown. Sew the units together into rows, and then join the rows to make a block measuring 6½" square, including seam allowances. Make a total of 83 Weathervane blocks.

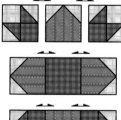
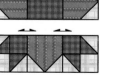
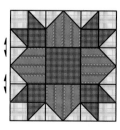

Make 83 blocks,
6½" × 6½".

Assembling and Finishing

For more help with any of the finishing steps, you'll find free information at ShopMartingale.com/HowtoQuilt.

1 Arrange the blocks, brown-stripe sashing strips, and cheddar cornerstones into diagonal rows as shown in the quilt assembly diagram below. Add the blue-and-brown check side and corner triangles.

2 Sew the blocks and sashing rectangles into diagonal rows as shown. Then join the cornerstones and sashing rectangles to make sashing strips.

3 Sew the block and sashing rows together and press. Add the corner triangles and press.

4 Trim the quilt top, leaving a ¼" seam allowance beyond the centers of the cornerstones and the corners of the sashing.

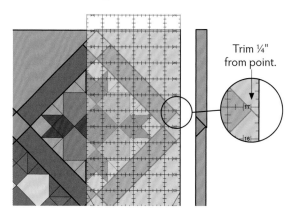

Trim ¼" from point.

5 Measure the length of the quilt top through the center and trim two of the dark brown check 6"-wide strips to this measurement. Sew the strips to the sides of the quilt and press.

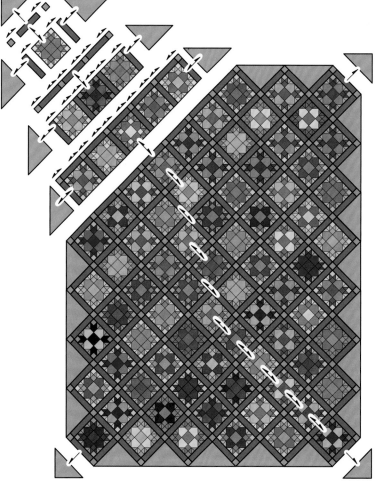

Quilt assembly

6 Measure the width of the quilt top through the center, including the just-added border pieces, and trim the two remaining dark brown check 6"-wide strips to this measurement. Sew the strips to the top and bottom of the quilt and press.

7 Layer the quilt top, batting, and backing. Baste the layers together and hand or machine quilt. The quilt shown is machine quilted with feathers and swirls in the blocks, a wavy line through the sashing, and a feather design in the border.

8 Trim the excess batting and backing fabric. Use the brown-and-tan 2"-wide strips to bind the quilt. Add a hanging sleeve, if desired, and a label.

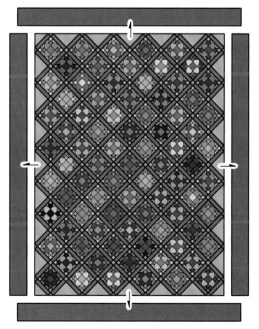

Adding borders

Waterfalls

One of the most popular hairstyles of the Civil War era was called "the waterfall," a look created by arranging a woman's hair into a flowing cascade down the back of her head. To create this style, according to Elizabeth McClellan in her book *Historic Dress in America: 1800–1870*, a public-domain document reprinted in 2015 by Sagwan Press, "A frame of horsehair was attached to the back of the head by an elastic, and the back hair brushed smoothly over it, the ends caught up underneath. A net was usually worn over this 'chignon' to keep the hair in place. Often the whole structure was made of false hair and fastened on with pins." Because this style was not easily held in place, it literally resulted in "fly away hair" on windy days!

FINISHED QUILT: 82⅝" × 82⅝" ✦ FINISHED BLOCK: 9" × 9"

Materials

Yardage is based on 42"-wide fabric. Fat quarters measure 18" x 21".

¾ yard *each* of 5 assorted light prints for blocks

13 fat quarters of assorted dark prints for blocks

3⅓ yards of blue-and-red stripe for sashing and border*

1½ yards of blue check for setting triangles

⅝ yard of navy print for binding

7½ yards of fabric for backing

91" × 91" piece of batting

*The border has mitered corners. If you prefer not to miter the corners, 3 yards is enough for the sashing and border.

To Add Interest

The key to achieving the strong graphic look of this quilt is to select fabrics for each block that clearly contrast with one another so that the nine-patch units are well defined and framed by adjacent triangles.

Cutting

Because the blocks in this quilt are so scrappy, and because a print may appear in different positions in different blocks, I recommend cutting fabrics for one block at a time. Repeat for a total of 25 blocks. All measurements include ¼"-wide seam allowances.

Cutting for Each Block (25 total)

From a light print, cut:

2 strips, 1½" × 16" (50 total)

3 squares, 3⅞" × 3⅞"; cut in half diagonally to yield 6 triangles (150 total)

From a dark print #1, cut:

3 squares, 3⅞" × 3⅞"; cut in half diagonally to yield 6 triangles (150 total)

From a dark print #2, cut:

1 strip, 1½" × 16" (25 total)

2 strips, 1½" × 8" (50 total)

From a dark print #3, cut:

1 strip, 1½" × 8" (25 total)

Continued on page 23

*Waterfalls, pieced by **Carol Hopkins** and quilted by **Lisa Ramsey***

Continued from page 21

Cutting for Sashing, Setting Triangles, and Border

From the *lengthwise* grain of the blue-and-red stripe, cut:*
4 strips, 5½" × 94"

From the *crosswise* grain of the *remaining* blue-and-red stripe, cut:
24 strips, 3½" × approximately 20"; crosscut into 48 strips, 3½" × 9½"
4 strips, 3½" × 42"; crosscut into 16 strips, 3½" × 9½"

From the blue check, cut:
2 strips, 18½" × 42"; crosscut into 3 squares, 18½" × 18½". Cut into quarters diagonally to yield 12 side triangles.
2 squares, 11¾" × 11¾"; cut in half diagonally to yield 4 corner triangles

From the navy print, cut:
9 strips, 2" × 42"

*For butted border corners, cut 4 lengthwise strips, 5½" × 84".

Making the Blocks

Instructions are for making one block at a time. Press the seam allowances as indicated by the arrows.

1 Sew light and dark #1 triangles together in pairs to make six matching half-square-triangle units measuring 3½" square, including seam allowances.

Make 6 units,
3½" × 3½".

2 Sew together one dark #2 and two matching light 1½" × 16" strips to make a strip set as shown. Crosscut the strip set into 10 segments measuring 1½" × 3½", including seam allowances.

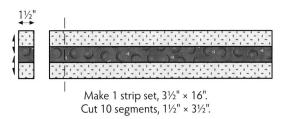

Make 1 strip set, 3½" × 16".
Cut 10 segments, 1½" × 3½".

3 Sew together two matching 1½" × 8" strips of dark #2 and one 1½" × 8" strip of dark #3 to make a strip set as shown. Crosscut the strip set into five segments measuring 1½" × 3½", including seam allowances.

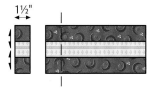

Make 1 strip set, 3½" × 8".
Cut 5 segments, 1½" × 3½".

4 Arrange and sew the segments from steps 2 and 3 into rows as shown. Sew the rows together to make a nine-patch unit measuring 3½" square, including seam allowances. Make a total of five nine-patch units; set two aside for later use in the sashing.

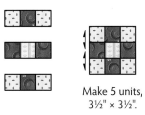

Make 5 units,
3½" × 3½".

5 Arrange the units from steps 1 and 4 as shown. Sew the units into rows, and then join the rows to make a block measuring 9½" square, including seam allowances. Make a total of 25 blocks.

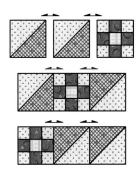 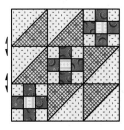

Make 25 blocks,
9½" × 9½".

Assembling and Finishing

For more help with any of the finishing steps, you'll find free information at ShopMartingale.com/HowtoQuilt.

1 Arrange the blocks, blue-and-red stripe sashing strips, and 40 of the nine-patch units into diagonal rows as shown in the quilt assembly diagram below. (You'll have 10 leftover nine-patch units.) Add the blue check side and corner triangles.

2 Sew the blocks and sashing rectangles into diagonal rows as shown. Then join the nine-patch cornerstones and sashing rectangles to make sashing strips.

3 Sew the block and sashing rows together and press after adding each row. Add the corner triangles and press.

4 Trim and square up the quilt top as needed, leaving a ¼" seam allowance beyond the corners of the nine-patch cornerstones.

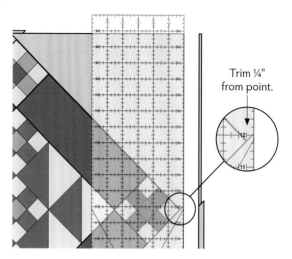

Trim ¼" from point.

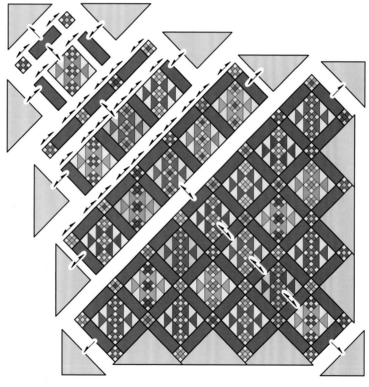

Quilt assembly

5 For mitered corners, center and sew a blue-and-red stripe 5½" × 94" strip to each side of the quilt, stopping ¼" from the end of each strip. Use your preferred method to miter the corners.

For butted corners, measure the length of the quilt top through the center and trim two of the blue-and-red stripe 5½" × 84" strips to this measurement. Sew the strips to the sides of the quilt and press. Measure the width of the quilt top through the center, including the just-added border pieces, and trim the two remaining blue-and-red stripe 5½" × 84" strips to this length. Sew the strips to the top and bottom of the quilt and press.

Adding borders

6 Layer the quilt top, batting, and backing. Baste the layers together and hand or machine quilt. The quilt shown is machine quilted with feathers and teardrops in the blocks, leaves and vines in the sashing, and a feather design in the border.

7 Trim the excess batting and backing fabric. Use the navy 2"-wide strips to bind the quilt. Add a hanging sleeve, if desired, and a label.

Mrs. Lincoln

Mary Todd Lincoln, First Lady of the United States from 1861–1865, was said to have guided President Lincoln in the social graces practiced in high society. Raised in a wealthy, aristocratic family dominated by a strict stepmother, Mrs. Lincoln was frequently criticized in public for being extravagant, particularly in her choice of lavish clothing during a time of war. However, her reputation grew steadily more positive as she engaged in tending to soldiers injured in battle.

FINISHED QUILT: 59" × 71½" ✦ **FINISHED BLOCK: 10" × 10"**

Materials

Yardage is based on 42"-wide fabric.

20 assorted light scraps, at least 13" × 14" each, for blocks
20 assorted dark scraps, at least 9" × 14" each, for blocks
⅔ yard of brown print for blocks
3 yards of pink-and-green stripe for sashing and border*
½ yard of olive print for binding
4⅓ yards of fabric for backing
65" × 78" piece of batting

*If you don't use a striped fabric, 2½ yards will be enough.

To Add Interest

Select a stripe containing design elements that can be isolated to create interesting horizontal sashing pieces.

Cutting

All measurements include ¼"-wide seam allowances.

From *each* of the light scraps, cut:
2 squares, 4" × 4"; cut into quarters diagonally to yield
   8 triangles (160 total)
1 square, 3¾" × 3¾" (20 total)
4 squares, 3" × 3" (80 total)
8 rectangles, 1¾" × 3" (160 total)
4 squares, 1¾" × 1¾" (80 total)

From *each* of the dark scraps, cut:
2 squares, 4" × 4"; cut into quarters diagonally to yield
   8 triangles (160 total)
1 square, 3" × 3" (20 total)
4 squares, 2⅛" × 2⅛" (80 total)
8 squares, 1¾" × 1¾" (160 total)

From the brown print, cut:
7 strips, 3" × 42"; crosscut into 80 squares, 3" × 3"

From the *lengthwise* grain of the pink-and-green stripe, cut:
4 matching strips, 6" × 62"
3 matching strips, 3" × 62"

From the *crosswise* grain of the remaining pink-and-green stripe, cut:*
6 matching strips, 3" × 42"; crosscut each strip into
   3 matching rectangles, 3" × 10½" (18 total, 2 are extra)

From the olive print, cut:
7 strips, 2" × 42"

*In order to create the effect of stripes in the sashing pieces from the top to the bottom of the quilt, cut the same segment of the stripe for each crosswise sashing piece.

Making the Blocks

Each block contains one light print, a dark print for the star, a second dark print for the outer ring of triangles, and the brown print for the block corners. Instructions are for making one block at a time. Press the seam allowances as indicated by the arrows.

27

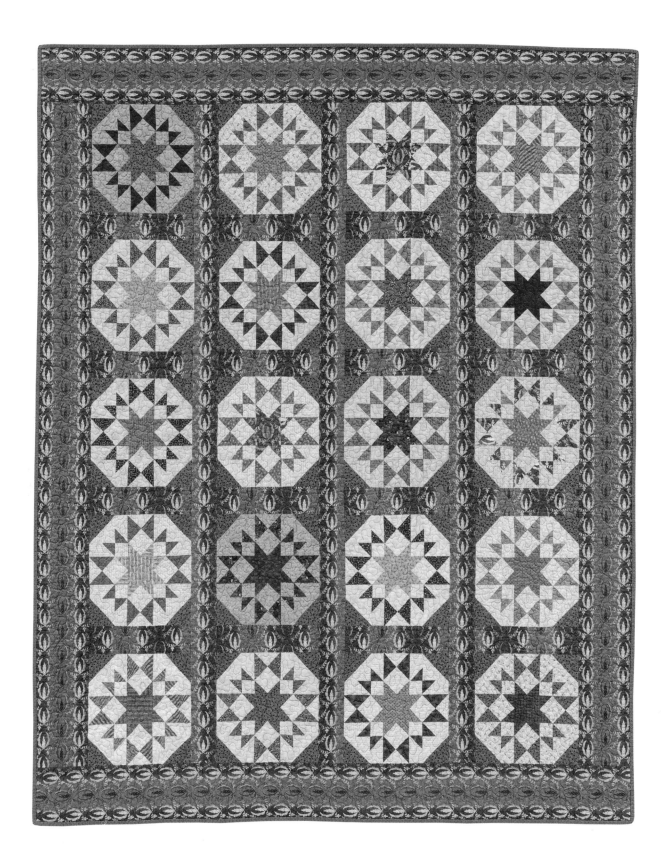

*Mrs. Lincoln, pieced by **Carol Hopkins** and quilted by **Lisa Ramsey***

1 To make four "no-waste" flying geese, mark a diagonal cutting line from corner to corner on the wrong side of four dark 2⅛" squares; mark diagonal sewing lines ¼" away from each side of this line.

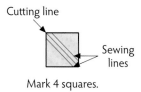

Cutting line

Sewing lines

Mark 4 squares.

2 With right sides together, place two of the marked squares on opposite corners of a light 3¾" square, overlapping slightly. Stitch along both marked sewing lines, and then cut the pieces apart along the cutting line and press.

3 Place a third marked square on the corner of the large triangle and stitch along the sewing lines. Cut the pieces apart along the cutting line. Repeat to make a total of four flying-geese units measuring 1¾" × 3", including seam allowances.

Make 4 units, 1¾" × 3".

4 Join dark and light 4" triangles in pairs along their short edges. Sew the pairs together to make four matching hourglass units. Trim the units to 3" square, including seam allowances.

Make 8 pairs.

3"

3"

Make 4 units.

5 Draw a diagonal line on the wrong side of eight matching dark 1¾" squares. Sew a square to the end of a light 1¾" × 3" rectangle, right sides together, as shown. Press the dark square toward the corner and trim the seam allowances to ¼" if desired. Make four units measuring 1¾" × 3", including seam allowances. In the same manner, make four additional units, noting the reversed position of the triangle.

Make 4 of each unit, 1¾" × 3".

6 Arrange four light 3" squares, four light 1¾" squares, and the units from steps 3, 4, and 5 as shown. Join the pieces into rows, and then sew the rows together.

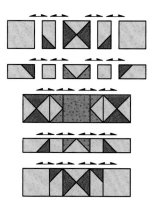

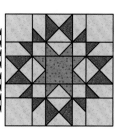

Make 1 block, 10½" × 10½".

7 Draw a diagonal line from corner to corner on the wrong side of four brown 3" squares. Sew a square to each corner of the block from step 6, right sides together. Press the brown square toward the corner and trim the seam allowances to ¼", if desired. Make 20 blocks measuring 10½" square, including seam allowances.

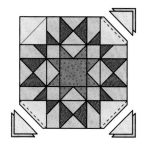 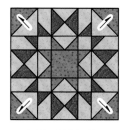

Make 20 blocks, 10½" × 10½".

Assembling and Finishing

For more help with any of the finishing steps, you'll find free information at ShopMartingale.com/HowtoQuilt.

1. Arrange the pieced blocks, the 3" × 10½" sashing pieces, and the 3" × 62" sashing strips as shown. Sew the blocks and sashing pieces into four vertical rows of five blocks and four sashing pieces each.

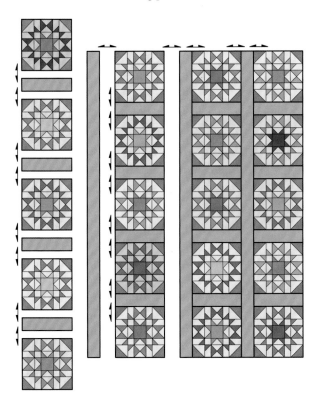

Quilt assembly

2. Measure the length of the rows and trim the three pink-and-green stripe 3"-wide sashing strips to that measurement; join the rows of blocks and sashing strips and press.

3. Measure the length of the quilt through the center and trim two pink-and-green stripe 6"-wide strips to this measurement. Sew the strips to the sides of the quilt and press.

4. Measure the width of the quilt top through the center, including the just-added border pieces, and trim the two remaining pink-and-green stripe 6"-wide strips to that length. Sew the strips to the top and bottom of the quilt and press.

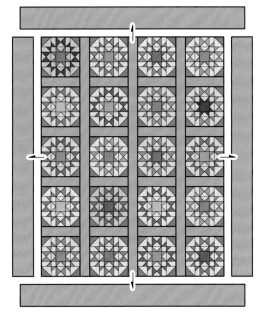

Adding borders

5. Layer the quilt top, batting, and backing. Baste the layers together and hand or machine quilt. The quilt shown is machine quilted with an allover stippling design.

6. Trim the excess batting and backing fabric. Use the olive 2"-wide strips to bind the quilt. Add a hanging sleeve, if desired, and a label.

Signals

Signal flags provided a means of communicating tactical and strategic information for Union and Confederate armies. From elevated signal stations, corpsmen communicated battlefield observations, intelligence gathering, and the direction of artillery fire. Seven cotton or linen flags of varying sizes and combinations of red, black, and white were available to provide optimal visibility in various weather and lighting conditions.

FINISHED QUILT: 49⅝" × 65½" ✦ FINISHED TRIANGLE BLOCK: 7½" × 7½" × 10½"

Materials

Yardage is based on 42"-wide fabric. Fat eighths measure 9" x 21".

12 fat eighths of assorted light prints for blocks

35 assorted medium or dark scraps (collectively referred to as "dark"), at least 4" × 6" *each*, for blocks

¼ yard *each* of 3 assorted red prints for blocks

1⅞ yards of medium brown print for setting triangles and binding

⅓ yard of tan print for inner border

1⅔ yards of dark brown print for outer border

4 yards of fabric for backing*

56" × 72" piece of batting

The backing yardage assumes a vertical seam. If you don't mind a horizontal seam, 3¼ yards will be enough.

To Add Interest

Select setting triangle and outer-border fabrics that are close in color, with subtle differences in the prints to add texture without interfering with the quilt's strong graphic design.

Cutting

All measurements include ¼"-wide seam allowances.

From *each* of the light prints, cut:
27 squares, 1¾" × 1¾" (324 total; 9 are extra)

From *each* of the dark prints, cut:
6 squares, 1¾" × 1¾" (210 total)

From *each* of the red prints, cut:
2 strips, 3" × 42"; crosscut into 18 squares, 3" × 3". Cut diagonally into quarters to yield 72 triangles (216 total; 2 of each print are extra).

From the medium brown print, cut:
4 strips, 11⅞" × 42"; crosscut into 11 squares, 11⅞" × 11⅞". Cut into quarters diagonally to yield 4 triangles (44 total; 2 are extra).
6 strips, 2" × 42" (for binding)

From the tan print, cut:
5 strips, 1½" × 42"

From the *lengthwise* grain of the dark brown print, cut:
4 strips, 5½" × 58"

Assembling and Finishing

For more help with any of the finishing steps, you'll find free information at ShopMartingale.com/HowtoQuilt.

1 Beginning with a medium brown triangle, sew together six brown triangles and five pieced blocks along the short sides of the triangles, alternating pieced and plain triangles. Do not line up the triangles edge to edge; instead, overlap the top triangle over the bottom triangle so that the bottom triangle point extends by ¼".

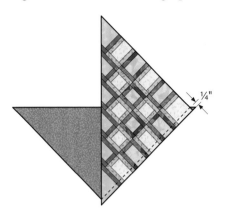

¼"

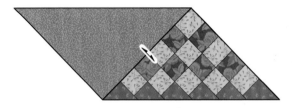

2 Press the seam allowances open after adding each triangle, being careful not to stretch the fabrics. The strip should end with a brown triangle. Make seven strips of 11 triangles.

Make 7 strips.

Making the Blocks

Each block contains one light, one dark, and one red fabric. Instructions are for making one block at a time. Press the seam allowances as indicated by the arrows.

Arrange nine matching light squares, six matching dark squares, and six matching red triangles in rows as shown. Sew the pieces into rows, and then join the rows to make a triangular block measuring 8⅜" along the short sides, and approximately 11⅞" along the long side. Repeat to make 35 blocks.

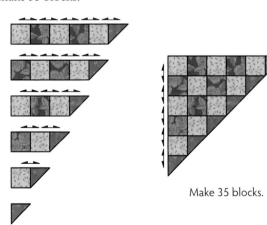

Make 35 blocks.

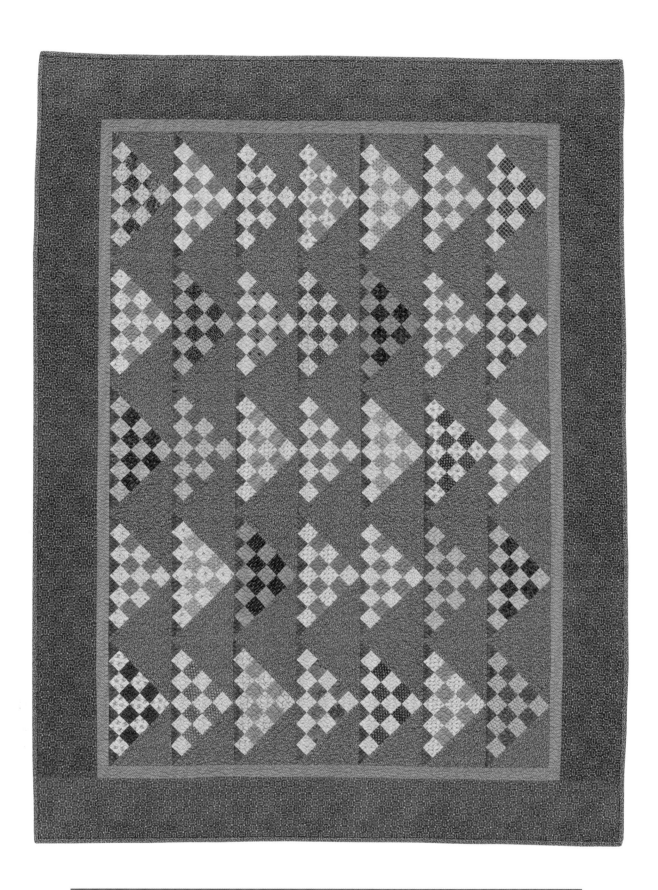

*Signals, pieced by **Carol Hopkins** and quilted by **Sue Hellenbrand***

3 Trim the brown triangles at the top and bottom of the triangle strips, leaving ¼" beyond the tip of the red triangle in the pieced block.

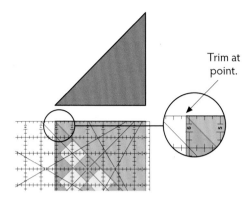

Trim at point.

4 Arrange the strips as shown, positioning the red triangles on the left side of each strip. Sew the strips together and press. Trim the top and bottom edges as needed, leaving ¼" beyond the red triangles in the pieced blocks.

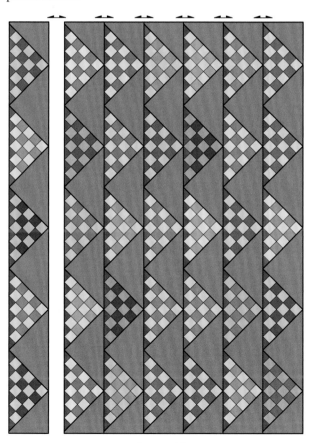

Quilt assembly

5 Sew the tan 1½"-wide strips together, end to end. For the inner border, measure the length of the quilt top through the center and cut two tan strips to this measurement. Sew the strips to the sides of the quilt and press.

6 Measure the width of the quilt top through the center, including the just-added border pieces, and cut two tan strips to this measurement. Sew the strips to the top and bottom of the quilt and press.

7 Repeat steps 5 and 6 without sewing the strips together, to add the dark brown 5½"-wide outer-border strips.

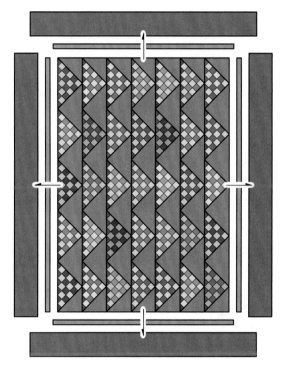

Adding borders

8 Layer the quilt top, batting, and backing. Baste the layers together and hand or machine quilt. The quilt shown is machine quilted with an allover stippling design.

9 Trim the excess batting and backing fabric. Use the medium brown 2"-wide strips to bind the quilt. Add a hanging sleeve, if desired, and a label.

Game of Graces

A popular 19th-century activity, deemed to be a proper and beneficial form of exercise for young girls, was known as "The Game of Graces." Opponents flung hoops decorated with beautiful pastel ribbons whirling toward each other to be caught on the tips of slender wands.

FINISHED QUILT: 60½" × 64½" ✦ FINISHED BLOCK: 4" × 4"

Materials

Yardage is based on 42"-wide fabric.

120 assorted light scraps, at least 6" × 6" *each,* for blocks*
120 assorted pink, blue, and brown scraps (collectively referred to as "dark"), at least 6" × 6" *each,* for blocks*
½ yard of blue print for binding
4 yards of fabric for backing
67" × 71" piece of batting

OR 4 yards total of assorted lights and 4 yards total of assorted darks.

To Add Interest

Use light prints containing designs of varying colors and densities. The quilt shown includes black, blue, brown, red, pink, and purple prints on a variety of off-white and cream-colored background fabrics.

Cutting

All measurements include ¼"-wide seam allowances.

From the light scraps, cut:
120 squares, 6" × 6"

From the dark scraps, cut:
120 squares, 6" × 6"

From the blue print, cut:
7 strips, 2" × 42"

Cutting the Triangles

Position a light square on top of a dark square, right sides together with edges aligned. Keeping the layers together, cut the squares into quarters diagonally, and then cut them in half vertically and horizontally to yield eight pairs of triangles. You'll have eight triangles from each fabric in the pair; 960 triangles total. Keep the layered triangles together for sewing and keep like fabrics together. You'll be making two Broken Dishes blocks from each pair of squares.

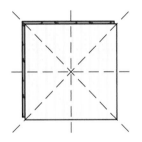 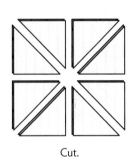

Cut.

Making the Blocks

Each block contains one light and one dark fabric. Instructions are for making one block. Press the seam allowances as indicated by the arrows.

1 Sew four matching pairs of light and dark triangles together to make four half-square-triangle units. Trim each unit to measure 2½" square, including seam allowances.

2½"

2½"

Make 4 units.

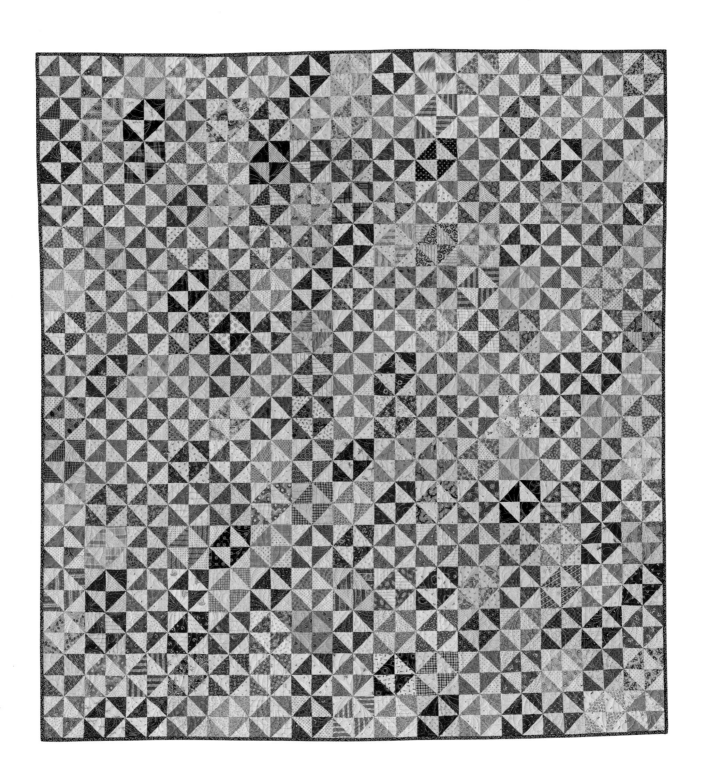

Game of Graces, pieced by Carol Hopkins and quilted by Marilyn Poppelwell

2 Arrange the half-square-triangle units as shown. Sew the units together into rows, and then join the rows to make a Broken Dishes block. Make 240 blocks measuring 4½" square, including seam allowances.

Make 240 blocks,
4½" × 4½".

Assembling and Finishing

For more help with any of the finishing steps, you'll find free information at ShopMartingale.com/HowtoQuilt.

1 Arrange the Broken Dishes blocks into 16 rows of 15 blocks each as shown, keeping all of the blocks oriented in the same direction. Sew the blocks into rows and press. Join the rows together and press after adding each row.

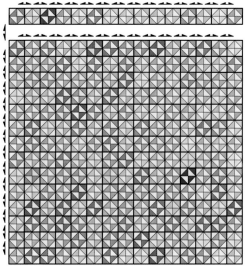

Quilt assembly

2 Layer the quilt top, batting, and backing. Baste the layers together and hand or machine quilt. The quilt shown is machine quilted with an allover swirling feather design.

3 Trim the excess batting and backing fabric. Use the blue 2"-wide strips to bind the quilt. Add a hanging sleeve, if desired, and a label.

Little Blue River

T he Little Blue River in Lexington, Missouri, was the site of the "Battle of the Little Blue," part of a plan to seize the state of Missouri for the Confederacy. The soldiers' mission was to destroy Union supplies and outposts in order to gain territory and harm Abraham Lincoln's chances for reelection in 1864.

FINISHED QUILT: 60" × 80½" ✦ FINISHED BLOCK: 7" × 7"

Materials

Yardage is based on 42"-wide fabric. Fat eighths measure 9" x 21".

¼ yard *each* of 8 light prints for blocks

16 fat eighths of assorted blue, red, green, and brown prints (collectively referred to as "dark"), for blocks

½ yard of yellow print for blocks

⅛ yard of pink print for blocks

2½ yards of blue floral print for setting triangles

2¼ yards of red print for outer border and binding*

5 yards of fabric for backing

66" × 87" piece of batting

*The yardage listed assumes binding strips are cut on the lengthwise grain. If you prefer to cut your binding crosswise, you'll need 2½ yards.

To Add Interest

When selecting light fabrics for the block backgrounds, include multicolored florals printed on light backgrounds to add color and movement to your blocks.

Cutting

All measurements include ¼"-wide seam allowances.

From *each* of the light prints, cut:

2 strips, 1½" × 42"; crosscut into:

    16 rectangles, 1½" × 2½" (128 total)

    16 squares, 1½" × 1½" (128 total)

1 strip, 1⅞" × 42"; crosscut into 16 squares, 1⅞" × 1⅞".

    Cut in half diagonally to yield 32 triangles (256 total).

From *each* of the dark prints, cut:

8 squares, 1⅞" × 1⅞; cut in half diagonally to yield

    16 triangles (256 total)

4 squares, 2⅞" × 2⅞"; cut in half diagonally to yield

    8 triangles (128 total)

8 rectangles, 1½" × 3½" (128 total)

From the yellow print, cut:

5 strips, 2⅞" × 42"; crosscut into 64 squares, 2⅞" × 2⅞".

    Cut in half diagonally to yield 128 triangles.

From the pink print, cut:

2 strips, 1½" × 42"; crosscut into 32 squares, 1½" × 1½"

From the blue floral print, cut:

6 strips, 11¼" × 42"; crosscut into 17 squares,

    11¼" × 11¼". Cut into quarters diagonally to yield 68

    setting triangles.

2 strips, 5⅞" × 42"; crosscut into 8 squares measuring

    5⅞" × 5⅞". Cut in half diagonally to yield 16 corner

    triangles.

From the *lengthwise* grain of the red print, cut:

4 strips, 5½" × 72"

4 strips, 2" × 72" (for binding)

Little Blue River, pieced by *Carol Hopkins* and quilted by *Lisa Ramsey*

Making the Blocks

Instructions are for making one block at a time. Press the seam allowances as indicated by the arrows.

1 Sew light and dark 1⅞" triangles together in pairs to make eight matching half-square-triangle units measuring 1½" square, including seam allowances.

Make 8 units,
1½" × 1½".

2 Sew yellow and dark 2⅞" triangles together in pairs to make four matching half-square-triangle units measuring 2½" square, including seam allowances.

Make 4 units,
2½" × 2½".

3 Join a light 1½" square and a 1½" half-square-triangle unit from step 1 as shown. Make a second unit, noting the reversed position of the triangle. Make two of each unit measuring 1½" × 2½", including seam allowances.

Make 2 of each unit,
1½" × 2½".

4 Join a light 1½" × 2½" rectangle and a 1½" half-square-triangle unit from step 1 as shown. Make a second unit, noting the reversed position of the triangle. Make two of each unit measuring 1½" × 3½", including seam allowances.

Make 2 of each unit,
1½" × 3½".

5 Arrange and sew the units from steps 2, 3, and 4 together as shown. Make a second unit, noting the reversed positions of the triangles. Make two of each unit measuring 3½" square, including seam allowances.

Make 2 of each unit,
3½" × 3½".

6 Arrange the units from step 5, four contrasting dark 1½" × 3½" rectangles, and a pink 1½" square as shown. Sew the pieces together into rows, and then join the rows to make a block measuring 7½" square, including seam allowances. Make 32 blocks.

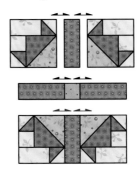 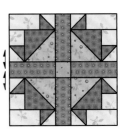

Make 32 blocks,
7½" × 7½".

Assembling and Finishing

For more help with any of the finishing steps, you'll find free information at ShopMartingale.com/HowtoQuilt.

1 Arrange five blocks, eight side triangles, and four corner triangles as shown. Sew the pieces into five diagonal units; press. Sew the units together and add two corner triangles to each end to complete one row A. Press. Repeat to make a total of four A rows that measure 10½" × 50".

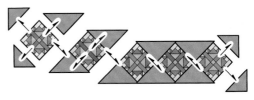

Row A.
Make 4 rows,
10½" × 50".

2 Arrange four blocks and 12 side triangles as shown. Sew the pieces into six diagonal units. Sew the units together to complete one row B. Press. Repeat to make a total of three B rows that measure 10½" × 50".

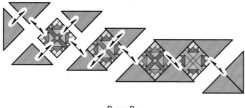

Row B.
Make 3 rows,
10½" × 50".

3 Sew the A and B rows together, alternating them as shown. Press after adding each row.

4 Measure the length of the quilt top through the center and trim two red 5½"-wide strips to this measurement. Sew the strips to the sides of the quilt and press the seam allowances toward the border.

5 Measure the width of the quilt top through the center, including the border strips just added, and trim the two remaining red 5½"-wide strips to that length. Sew the strips to the top and bottom of the quilt and press the seam allowances toward the border.

6 Layer the quilt top, batting, and backing. Baste the layers together and hand or machine quilt. The quilt shown is machine quilted with swirls, leaves, and vines in the blocks and feather designs in the setting triangles and border.

7 Trim the excess batting and backing. Use the red 2"-wide strips to bind the quilt. Add a hanging sleeve, if desired, and a label.

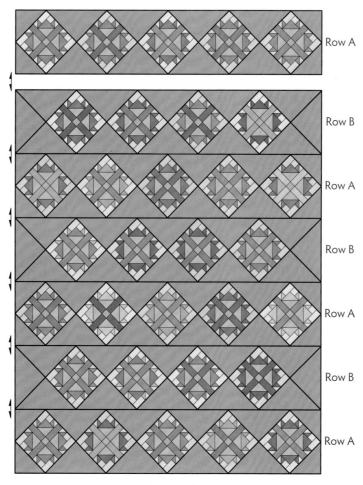

Row A

Row B

Row A

Row B

Row A

Row B

Row A

Quilt assembly

Nellie Jane

My husband's paternal grandmother was named Nellie. His maternal grandmother's middle name was Jane. I blended the families to create the name of this quilt. The consistent structure of the Hourglass blocks reflects Nellie's highly organized household. The shifting directions of the sashing triangles capture Rebecca Jane's life with six children.

FINISHED QUILT: 54" × 75¼" ✦ FINISHED BLOCK: 6" × 6"

Materials

Yardage is based on 42"-wide fabric.

20 assorted light scraps, at least 8" × 8" *each*, for blocks

20 assorted red, pink, gold, cheddar, blue, and brown scraps (collectively referred to as "dark"), at least 8" × 8" *each*, for blocks

56 assorted light scraps, 5" × 5" *each*, for sashing triangles

56 assorted dark scraps, 5" × 5" *each*, for sashing triangles

¾ yard of tan check for setting triangles

2 yards of brown print for border

½ yard of brown-and-tan print for binding

4⅝ yards of fabric for backing

60" × 82" piece of batting

To Add Interest

Showcase your favorite prints in the large Hourglass blocks. Include lots of plaids, checks, and stripes to give this quilt a warm, worn-and-loved look.

Cutting

All measurements include ¼"-wide seam allowances.

From *each* of the light 8" scraps, cut:
1 square, 7¼" × 7¼"; cut into quarters diagonally to yield 4 triangles (80 total, 2 are extra)

From *each* of the dark 8" scraps, cut:
1 square, 7¼" × 7¼"; cut into quarters diagonally to yield 4 triangles (80 total, 2 are extra)

From *each* of the light 5" squares, cut:
8 triangles by cutting into quarters diagonally and again horizontally and vertically (448 total, 6 are extra)

From *each* of the dark 5" squares, cut:
8 triangles by cutting into quarters diagonally and again horizontally and vertically (448 total, 6 are extra)

From the tan check, cut:
2 strips, 12" × 42"; crosscut into 4 squares, 12" × 12"; cut into quarters diagonally to yield 16 side triangles.
2 squares, 7¼" × 7¼"; cut in half diagonally to yield 4 corner triangles

From the *lengthwise* grain of the brown print, cut:
4 strips, 5" × 70"

From the brown-and-tan print, cut:
7 strips, 2" × 42"

45

Making the Blocks and Sashing

1 Arrange two matching light and two matching dark 7¼" triangles as shown. Sew the pieces together in pairs, and then join the pairs. Make 39 Hourglass blocks measuring 6½" square, including seam allowances.

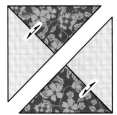 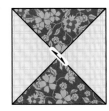

Make 39 units,
6½" × 6½".

2 Sew small light and dark triangles together in pairs to make 442 half-square-triangle units. Trim each unit to 2" square, including seam allowances.

Make 442 units.

3 Sew together four half-square-triangle units to make a sashing strip measuring 2" × 6½", including seam allowances. Make 48 sashing strips. Repeat to make 48 additional sashing strips, reversing the positions of the triangles. Set aside the remaining 58 half-square-triangle units to use as cornerstones.

Make 48 of each unit,
2" × 6½".

Assembling and Finishing

For more help with any of the finishing steps, you'll find free information at ShopMartingale.com/HowtoQuilt.

1 Arrange the Hourglass blocks, sashing strips, and half-square-triangle cornerstones into diagonal rows as shown in the quilt assembly diagram below, paying close attention to the position of the triangles in the sashing strips and cornerstones. Add the tan check side and corner triangles.

2 Sew the blocks and sashing pieces into diagonal rows as shown. Then join the cornerstones and sashing rectangles to make sashing rows.

3 Sew the block rows and sashing rows together and press. Add the corner triangles and press.

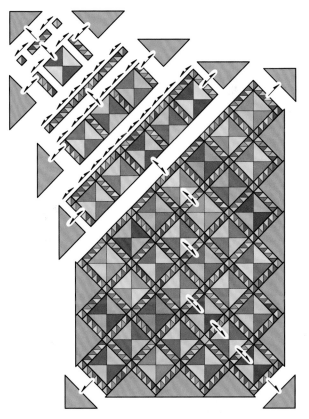

Quilt assembly

4 Measure the length of the quilt top through the center and trim two of the brown 5"-wide strips to this measurement. Sew the strips to the sides of the quilt and press.

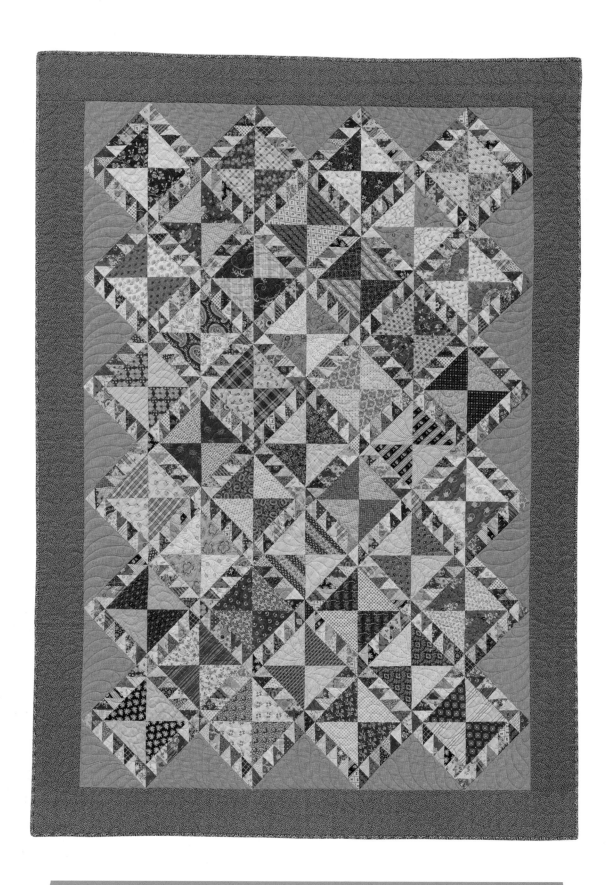

Nellie Jane, pieced by **Carol Hopkins** *and quilted by* **Carol Alberts**

5 Measure the width of the quilt top through the center, including the just-added border pieces, and trim the two remaining brown strips to this measurement. Sew the strips to the top and bottom of the quilt and press.

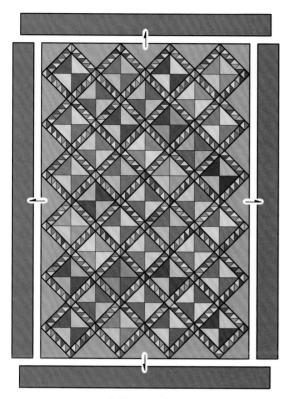

Adding borders

6 Layer the quilt top, batting, and backing. Baste the layers together and hand or machine quilt. The quilt shown is machine quilted with a variety of feather designs in the blocks, setting triangles, and outer border.

7 Trim the excess batting and backing fabric. Use the brown-and-tan 2"-wide strips to bind the quilt. Add a hanging sleeve, if desired, and a label.

Faded Roses

Poems written by Confederate soldiers in the midst of war were cataloged by Esther Parker Ellinger in her 1918 doctoral dissertation from the University of Pennsylvania. "Loved and Lost" by Colonel B. H. Jones begins:

> *"I have a rose—a faded rose,*
> *Sweeter than many a fairer flower."*

FINISHED QUILT: 60½" × 60½" ✦ FINISHED BLOCK: 4" × 4"

Materials

Yardage is based on 42"-wide fabric.

144 assorted light scraps, at least 6" × 7" *each*, for block backgrounds

144 assorted pink and brown scraps (collectively referred to as "dark"), at least 7" × 7" *each*, for stars

1⅞ yards of brown floral print for border

½ yard of pink-and-brown print for binding

3¾ yards of fabric for backing

67" × 67" piece of batting

To Add Interest

Select pinks ranging from pale pink to dark burgundy, browns ranging from bronze to chocolate, lights with lots of pattern and colorful prints, and then sprinkle in a few green prints for good measure. Make a few twinkling stars by reversing the position of light and dark prints in some of the blocks.

Cutting

All measurements include ¼"-wide seam allowances.

From *each* of the light scraps, cut:
4 rectangles, 1½" × 2½" (576 total)
4 squares, 1½" × 1½" (576 total)

From *each* of the dark scraps, cut:
1 square, 2½" × 2½" (144 total)
8 squares, 1½" × 1½" (1152 total)

From the *lengthwise* grain of the brown floral print, cut:
4 strips, 6½" × 64"

From the pink-and-brown print, cut:
7 strips, 2" × 42"

Making the Blocks

Each Star block contains a light and a dark print. Instructions are for making one block. Press the seam allowances as indicated by the arrows.

1 Draw a diagonal line from corner to corner on the wrong side of eight matching dark 1½" squares. Place a marked square on one end of a light 1½" × 2½" rectangle with right sides together as shown. Stitch along the drawn line and then trim the seam allowances to ¼" if desired. Press. Stitch, trim, and press a marked square to the other end of the same rectangle. Make four units measuring 1½" × 2½", including seam allowances.

Make 4 units,
1½" × 2½".

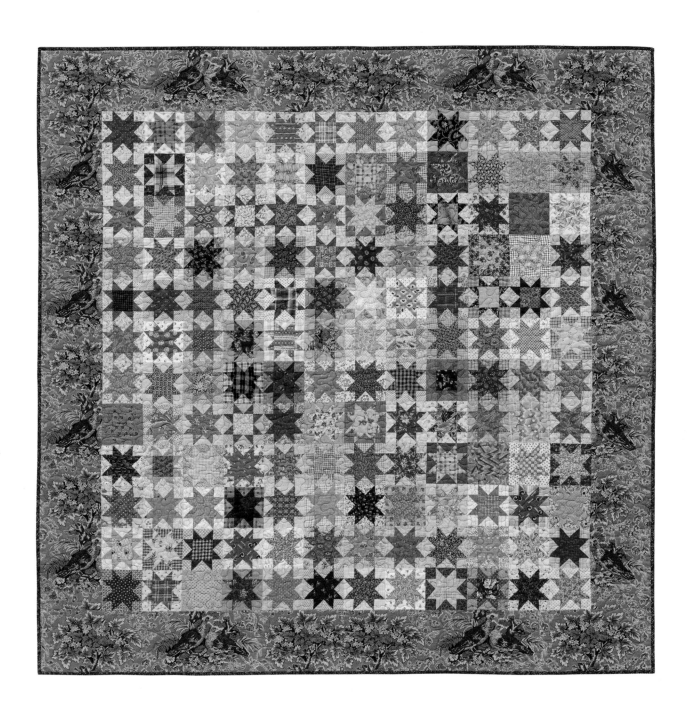

Faded Roses, pieced by Carol Hopkins and quilted by Lisa Ramsey

2 Arrange four matching light 1½" squares, the units from step 1, and a matching dark 2½" square as shown. Sew the pieces together into rows, and then join the rows to make a Star block measuring 4½" square, including seam allowances. Make 144 Star blocks.

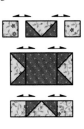

Make 144 blocks,
4½" × 4½".

Assembling and Finishing

For more help with any of the finishing steps, you'll find free information at ShopMartingale.com/HowtoQuilt.

1 Arrange the Star blocks into 12 rows of 12 blocks each as shown below. Sew the blocks into rows and press. Join the rows and press.

2 Measure the length of the quilt top through the center and trim two of the brown floral 6½"-wide strips to this measurement. Sew the strips to the sides of the quilt top and press seam allowances toward the border.

3 Measure the width of the quilt top through the center, including the just-added border pieces, and cut the two remaining brown floral 6½"-wide strips to this

measurement. Sew the strips to the top and bottom of the quilt top and press seam allowances toward the border.

4 Layer the quilt top, batting, and backing. Baste the layers together and hand or machine quilt. The center of the quilt shown is machine quilted with an overall meandering design, and the border is quilted with a feather design.

5 Trim the excess batting and backing fabric. Use the pink-and-brown 2"-wide strips to bind the quilt. Add a hanging sleeve, if desired, and a label.

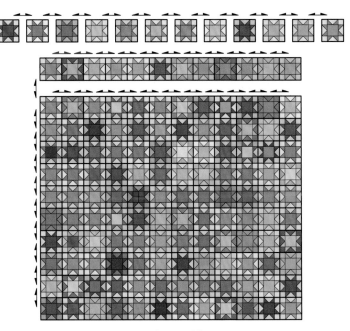

Quilt assembly

Southern Belles

The rich dark browns, bright poison greens, madder prints, and highly detailed stripe fabrics used in this medallion-style quilt are accurate reproductions of colors and prints available during the mid-1860s. Just imagine the lovely dresses these fabrics would have made.

FINISHED QUILT: 53½" × 53½" ✦ FINISHED BLOCKS: 6" × 6" AND 4½" × 4½"

Materials

Yardage is based on 42"-wide fabric.

1⅓ yards of dark brown print for blocks, pieced border 3, and binding
½ yard of light print for blocks
4 assorted red or tan scraps, at least 4" × 4" *each*, for blocks
⅜ yard of rust print for center block and border 2
⅞ yard of tan print for blocks and pieced border 3
1⅔ yards of large-scale floral for medallion center and border 5
¼ yard of green print for blocks and border 1
1⅛ yards of rust stripe for border 4
3⅓ yards of fabric for backing
60" × 60" piece of batting

To Add Interest

Make fabric selection for this quilt easy by choosing coordinating prints from a single fabric line that includes wide stripes, large florals, and coordinating light, medium, and dark prints.

Cutting

All measurements include ¼"-wide seam allowances.

From the dark brown print, cut:
4 strips, 3½" × 42"; crosscut into 44 squares, 3½" × 3½"
3 strips, 2" × 42"; crosscut into 44 squares, 2" × 2"
2 squares, 7¼" × 7¼"; cut into quarters diagonally to yield 8 triangles
2 strips, 1⅝" × 42"; crosscut into 32 squares, 1⅝" × 1⅝"
6 strips, 2" × 42" (for binding)

From the light print, cut:
3 strips, 2" × 42"; crosscut into:
    20 rectangles, 2" × 3½"
    20 squares, 2" × 2"
1 square, 7¼" × 7¼"; cut into quarters diagonally to yield 4 triangles

From *each* of the assorted red or tan scraps, cut:
1 square, 3½" × 3½" (4 total)

From the rust print, cut:
1 square, 3½" × 3½"
4 strips, 2" × 27½"

From the tan print, cut:
1 square, 7¼" × 7¼"; cut into quarters diagonally to yield 4 triangles
4 strips, 3½" × 42"; crosscut into 20 rectangles, 3½" × 6½"
2 strips, 1⅝" × 42"; crosscut into:
    16 rectangles, 1⅝" × 2¾"
    16 squares, 1⅝" × 1⅝"

Continued on page 57

*Southern Belles, pieced by **Carol Hopkins** and quilted by **Lisa Ramsey***

Continued from page 55

From the *lengthwise* grain of the large-scale floral, cut:
2 strips, 4½" × 45½"
2 strips, 4½" × 53½"

From the *remainder* of the large-scale floral, cut:
2 squares, 13⅝" × 13⅝"; cut in half diagonally to yield
 4 triangles

From the green print, cut:
2 strips, 1¼" × 26"
2 strips, 1¼" × 27½"
4 squares, 2¾" × 2¾"

From the *lengthwise* grain of the rust stripe, cut:
4 strips, 5" × 36½"

Making the Medallion Center

Press the seam allowances as indicated by the arrows.

1 Make a flying-geese unit with two dark brown 2"
 squares and one light 2" × 3½" rectangle as shown.
Make 20 matching units.

Make 20 units,
2" × 3½".

2 Arrange four flying-geese units, four light 2" squares,
 and one red, tan, or rust 3½" square as shown. Sew
the pieces into rows, and then sew the rows together.
Make five Star blocks measuring 6½" square, including
seam allowances.

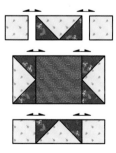 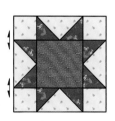

Make 5 blocks,
6½" × 6½".

3 Repeat step 1 using dark brown 1⅝" squares and tan
 1⅝" × 2¾" rectangles to make 16 flying-geese units.
Repeat step 2 using the flying-geese units, green 2¾"
squares, and tan 1⅝" squares. Make four Star blocks that
measure 5" square, including seam allowances. Set these
blocks aside for border assembly.

Make 4 blocks,
5" × 5".

4 Sew together two dark brown triangles, one tan
 triangle, and one light triangle as shown to make an
Hourglass block measuring 6½" square, including seam
allowances. Make four.

Make 4 blocks,
6½" × 6½".

5 Arrange the 6½" Star blocks and Hourglass blocks as
 shown. Sew the blocks into rows; press. Join the rows
and press after adding each row to make the medallion
center measuring 18½" square, including seam allowances.

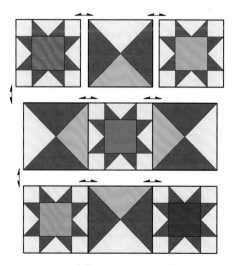

Medallion center assembly

6 Sew floral triangles to opposite sides of the medallion center. Sew matching triangles to the remaining sides of the unit to complete the medallion, which should measure 26" square, including seam allowances.

Make 1 unit,
26" × 26".

Making and Adding the Borders

1 Sew the green 1¼" × 26" strips to opposite sides of the quilt center. Sew the green 1¼" × 27½" strips to the top and bottom of the quilt center. The quilt top should now measure 27½" square, including seam allowances.

2 Sew rust 2" × 27½" strips to opposite sides of the quilt center. Sew a dark brown 2" square to each end of the two remaining rust 2" × 27½" strips. Sew these strips to the top and bottom of the quilt center. The quilt top should now measure 30½" square, including seam allowances.

3 Make a flying-geese unit with two dark brown 3½" squares and one tan 3½" × 6½" rectangle. Make 20 units measuring 3½" × 6½", including seam allowances.

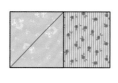 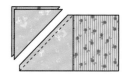
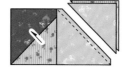 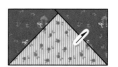

Make 20 units,
3½" × 6½".

4 Sew five flying-geese units together end to end to make a pieced border. Make four strips. Sew two of the flying-geese strips to opposite sides of the quilt top. Sew a dark brown 3½" square to each end of the two remaining flying-geese strips. Sew these strips to the top and bottom of the quilt. The quilt top should now measure 36½" square, including seam allowances.

Make 2 side borders,
3½" × 30½".

Make 2 top/bottom borders,
3½" × 36½".

5 Sew rust striped 5" × 36½" strips to opposite sides of the quilt top. Sew a 5" Star block to each end of the two remaining rust-striped 5" × 36½" strips. Sew these strips to the top and bottom of the quilt. The quilt top should now measure 45½" square, including seam allowances.

6 Sew the floral 4½" × 45½" strips to the sides of the quilt. Sew the 4½" × 53½" strips to the top and bottom of the quilt. The quilt top should measure 53½" square.

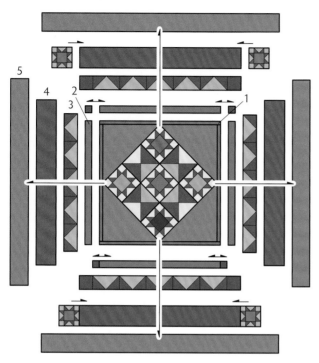

Adding borders

Finishing

For more help with any of the finishing steps, you'll find free information at ShopMartingale.com/HowtoQuilt.

1 Layer the quilt top, batting, and backing. Baste the layers together and hand or machine quilt. The quilt shown is machine quilted with floral motifs in the center block and pieced border. The striped border is quilted lengthwise along the various sections of the stripe, and the outer border is quilted with feathers.

2 Trim the excess batting and backing fabric. Use the dark brown 2"-wide strips to bind the quilt. Add a hanging sleeve, if desired, and a label.

Changing Colors

T he blue and gray colors of Northern and Southern soldiers' uniforms changed as they became faded, worn, and dirty throughout the course of the Civil War. This quilt was inspired by those uniforms and a photograph of an antique quilt.

FINISHED QUILT: 50⅝" × 62⅜" ✦ FINISHED BLOCK: 5⅞" × 5⅞"

Materials

Yardage is based on 42"-wide fabric.

32 assorted light scraps, at least 5" × 7" *each*, for blocks

32 assorted dark scraps, at least 8" × 10" *each*, for blocks

1¼ yards of gray-and-taupe stripe for setting squares

1⅔ yards of gray print for border and binding*

3⅞ yards of fabric for backing

57" × 69" piece of batting

The yardage listed assumes binding strips are cut on the lengthwise grain. If you prefer to cut your binding crosswise, you'll need 2 yards.

To Add Interest

Break away from beige and select a light pink, blue, or gray for some of the block backgrounds. Use two different dark fabrics for the large and small triangles in some of the blocks.

Cutting

All measurements include ¼"-wide seam allowances.

From *each* of the light scraps, cut:

6 squares, 2¼" × 2¼"; cut in half diagonally to yield 12 triangles (384 total)

From *each* of the dark scraps, cut:

3 squares, 2¼" × 2¼"; cut in half diagonally to yield 6 triangles (192 total)

1 square, 7¼" × 7¼"; cut into quarters diagonally to yield 4 triangles (128 total, 64 are extra)*

From the gray-and-taupe stripe, cut:**

6 strips, 6½" × 42"; crosscut into 31 squares, 6½" × 6½"

From the *lengthwise* grain of the gray print, cut:

4 strips, 5" × 54"

5 strips, 2" × 54" (for binding)

The 7¼" square is cut slightly oversized; excess will be trimmed when the block is squared up.

**It's best to wait until after making the pieced blocks to cut these squares. Measure the pieced blocks and cut the setting squares to match the size of your blocks.*

Making the Blocks

Each block contains one light and one dark fabric. Instructions are for making one block at a time. Press the seam allowances as indicated by the arrows.

1 Sew light and dark 2¼" triangles together in pairs to make six matching half-square-triangle units measuring 1⅞" square, including seam allowances.

Make 6 units,
1⅞" × 1⅞".

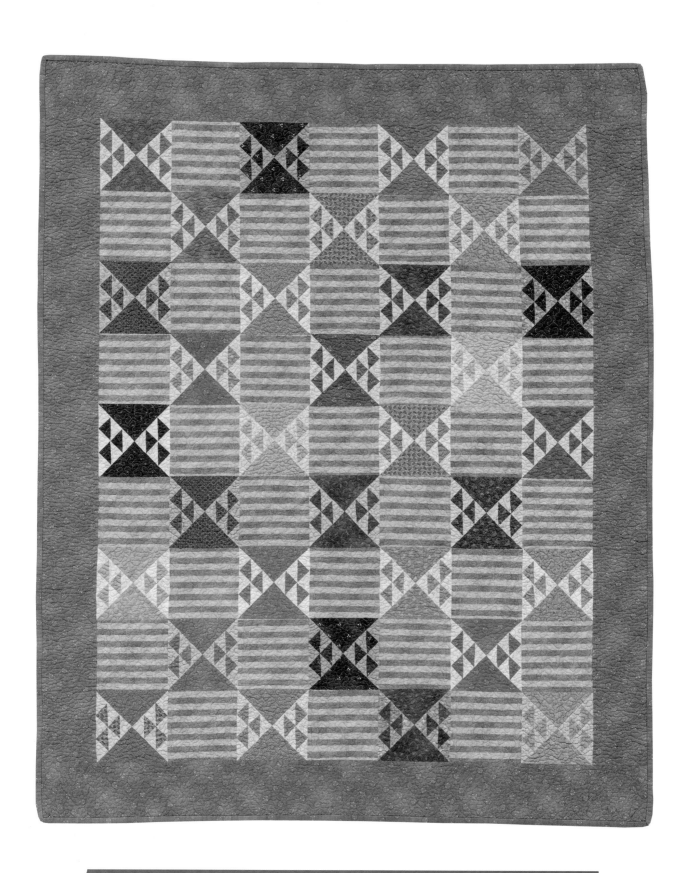

*Changing Colors, pieced by **Carol Hopkins** and quilted by **Sue Hellenbrand***

2 Arrange three light 2¼" triangles and three half-square-triangle units as shown. Sew the pieces together into rows, and then join the rows. Repeat to make two matching units. Handle the units carefully so as not to distort the bias edges.

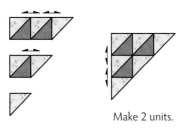

Make 2 units.

3 Arrange the units from step 2 and two matching 7¼" dark triangles as shown. Sew the pieces together into rows, and then join the rows together. Repeat to make a total of 32 blocks.

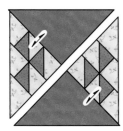 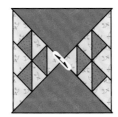

Make 32 blocks.

4 Square up the blocks, leaving a ¼" seam allowance beyond the points of the small triangles. The blocks should measure approximately 6⅜" square, including seam allowances. Don't worry if your blocks are a slightly different size. Trim them to a uniform size and cut the gray-and-taupe striped alternate blocks to that size.

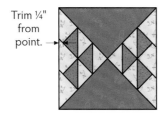

Trim ¼" from point. →

Assembling and Finishing

For more help with any of the finishing steps, you'll find free information at ShopMartingale.com/HowtoQuilt.

1 Arrange the blocks and the striped setting squares in nine rows of seven units each, alternating them as shown in the quilt assembly diagram below. Sew the units together into rows; press. Join the rows together and press.

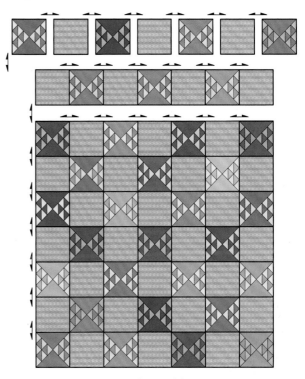

Quilt assembly

2 Measure the length of the quilt top through the center and trim two of the gray 5"-wide strips to this measurement. Sew the strips to the sides of the quilt and press. Measure the width of the quilt top through the center, including the just-added border pieces, and trim the two remaining gray 5"-wide strips to this measurement. Sew the strips to the top and bottom of the quilt and press.

3 Layer the quilt top, batting, and backing. Baste the layers together and hand or machine quilt. The quilt shown is machine quilted with feathers and swirls in the blocks, a wavy line through the sashing, and a feather design in the border.

4 Trim the excess batting and backing fabric. Use the gray 2"-wide strips to bind the quilt. Add a hanging sleeve, if desired, and a label.

Juliet's Ribbons

Nurse Juliet Opie Hopkins (no relation) used the proceeds from selling her estates in New York, Virginia, and Alabama to establish hospitals for sick and wounded soldiers. While there is no mention of her having been a quilter, she did have the carpets in her homes cut up to make blankets for soldiers. Sadly, Julia lost all of her money during the Civil War and lived the rest of her life in poverty. However, because her philanthropic efforts were so greatly appreciated, she was buried with full military honors at Arlington National Cemetery.

FINISHED QUILT: 54⅞" × 59" ✦ **FINISHED BLOCK: 5" × 5"**

Materials

Yardage is based on 42"-wide fabric.

35 assorted light scraps, at least 7" × 8" *each*, for blocks

35 assorted red, pink, blue, brown, and black scraps (collectively referred to as "dark"), at least 5" × 11" *each*, for blocks

1⅓ yards of blue print for setting triangles

1⅝ yards of tan stripe for sashing*

1⅞ yards of red-and-blue print for borders

½ yard of red-and-black print for binding

3⅔ yards of fabric for backing

61" × 65" piece of batting

*If you use a nondirectional print rather than a stripe, ⅝ yard will be enough.

To Add Interest

Instead of using the same light fabric for the block background and small center square, use a dark fabric in some of the block centers.

Cutting

All measurements include ¼"-wide seam allowances.

From *each* of the light scraps, cut:
17 squares, 1½" × 1½" (595 total)

From *each* of the dark scraps, cut:
4 squares, 2½" × 2½" (140 total)
4 rectangles, 1½" × 2½" (140 total)

From the blue print, cut:
4 strips, 8½" × 42"; crosscut into 15 squares, 8½" × 8½". Cut into quarters diagonally to yield 60 setting triangles.
2 strips, 4½" × 42"; crosscut into 10 squares, 4½" × 4½". Cut in half diagonally to yield 20 corner triangles.

From the *lengthwise* grain of the tan stripe, cut:*
4 strips, 3" × 52"

From the *lengthwise* grain of the red-and-blue print, cut:
4 strips, 5" × 58"

From the red-and-black print, cut:
6 strips, 2" × 42"

*For a tan nondirectional print, cut 6 strips, 3" × 42", from the crosswise grain.

Juliet's Ribbons, pieced by Carol Hopkins and quilted by Lisa Ramsey

Making the Blocks

Instructions are for making one block. Press all seam allowances as indicated by the arrows.

1 Place a light 1½" square on one corner of a dark 2½" square, right sides together. Sew diagonally across the light square. Fold the resulting light triangle toward the outer corner and press in place; trim the seam allowances to ¼" if desired. Sew matching light squares on the remaining three corners of the same dark square, pressing after adding each square. Make four matching square-in-a square units measuring 2½" square, including seam allowances.

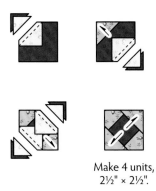

Make 4 units,
2½" × 2½".

2 Arrange the square-in-a-square units, four contrasting dark 1½" × 2½" rectangles, and a light (or a different dark print) 1½" square as shown. Sew the pieces into rows, and then join the rows. Repeat to make 35 blocks measuring 5½" square, including seam allowances.

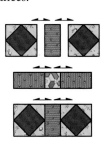 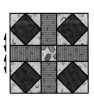

Make 35 blocks,
5½" × 5½".

Assembling and Finishing

For more help with any of the finishing steps, you'll find free information at ShopMartingale.com/HowtoQuilt.

1 Sew seven blocks and 12 blue 8½" triangles together as shown to make a vertical row. Make five rows.

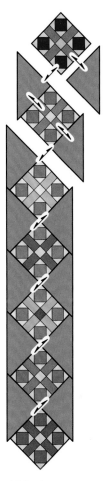

Make 5 rows.

2 Add blue 4½" triangles to the corners of the rows and press.

3 Trim the rows, leaving ¼" beyond the points of the blocks for seam allowance.

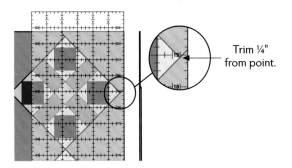

Trim ¼"
from point.

4 Measure the length of the rows from step 2 and trim the four tan-stripe strips to this measurement.

5 Arrange the rows and tan-stripe strips as shown below. Sew the rows and strips together; press after adding each strip.

6 Measure the length of the quilt top through the center and trim two red-and-blue 5"-wide strips to this measurement. Sew the strips to the sides of the quilt and press. Measure the width of the quilt top through the center, including the just-added border pieces, and trim

the two remaining red-and-blue 5"-wide strips to this measurement. Sew the strips to the top and bottom of the quilt and press.

7 Layer the quilt top, batting, and backing. Baste the layers together and hand or machine quilt. The quilt shown is machine quilted with swirls in the block rectangles, half circles in the sashing strips, and feather designs in the setting triangles and border.

8 Trim the excess batting and backing fabric. Use the red-and-black 2"-wide strips to bind the quilt. Add a hanging sleeve, if desired, and a label.

Quilt assembly

Give and Take

I f you look up the expression "give and take," you'll find phrases like happy relationship, mutual interaction, reciprocating, exchanging, mutually productive, shared benefits, cooperation, and free-flowing exchange. All of these are perfect descriptions of the yearlong block exchange with three of my friends. As in previous exchanges, we selected a simple block, and this quilt is the result.

FINISHED QUILT: 70" × 91¼" ✦ FINISHED BLOCK: 5" × 5"

Materials

Yardage is based on 42"-wide fabric.

83 assorted light scraps, at least 5" × 8" *each*, for blocks
83 assorted dark scraps, at least 3" × 6" *each*, for blocks
83 assorted dark scraps, at least 3" × 3" *each*, for blocks
3⅛ yards of dark gray print for setting triangles
⅜ yard of light gray print for inner border
2½ yards of gray-and-tan print for outer border
⅝ yard of gray dot print for binding
5½ yards of fabric for backing
78" × 100" piece of batting

To Add Interest

It's the scrappy variety of fabrics that make the blocks in this quilt sparkle among the dark zigzag setting triangles. A good system for selecting fabrics for this quilt is to dig into your scrap bag for prints of various colors and sizes. Select a calming tone-on-tone print for the zigzag setting pieces to showcase, but not compete with, the fabrics in each block.

Cutting

All measurements include ¼"-wide seam allowances.

From *each* of the light scraps, cut:
5 squares, 1½" × 1½" (415 total)
2 squares, 2⅞" × 2⅞"; cut in half diagonally to yield
    4 triangles (332 total)

From *each* of the 3" × 6" dark scraps, cut:
2 squares, 2⅞" × 2⅞"; cut in half diagonally to yield
    4 triangles (332 total)

From *each* of the 3" × 3" dark scraps, cut:
4 squares, 1½" × 1½" (332 total)

From the dark gray print, cut:
11 strips, 8⅜" × 42"; crosscut into 44 squares, 8⅜" × 8⅜".
    Cut into quarters diagonally to yield 176 triangles
    (2 are extra).
2 strips, 4½" × 42"; crosscut into 12 squares, 4½" × 4½".
    Cut in half diagonally to yield 24 corner triangles.

From the light gray print, cut:
7 strips, 1½" × 42"

From the *lengthwise* grain of the gray-and-tan print, cut:
4 strips, 6" × 82"

From the gray dot print, cut:
9 strips, 2" × 42"

Making the Blocks

Instructions are for making one block. Press the seam allowances as indicated by the arrows.

1 Sew light and dark 2⅞" triangles together in pairs to make four matching half-square-triangle units measuring 2½" square, including seam allowances.

Make 4 units,
2½" × 2½".

2 Sew light and contrasting dark 1½" squares together to make four matching units measuring 1½" × 2½", including seam allowances.

Make 4 units,
1½" × 2½".

3 Arrange a matching light 1½" square and the units from steps 1 and 2 as shown. Sew the pieces into rows, and then join the rows together. Make 83 blocks measuring 5½" square, including seam allowances.

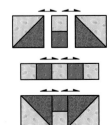

Make 83 blocks,
5½" × 5½".

Assembling and Finishing

For more help with any of the finishing steps, you'll find free information at ShopMartingale.com/HowtoQuilt.

1 Arrange eight blocks, 14 side triangles, and four corner triangles as shown. Sew the pieces into eight diagonal units; press. Join the units together and add two corner triangles to each end to complete row A. Press. Make a total of six A rows.

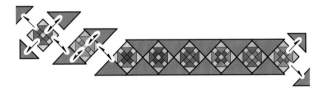

Row A.
Make 6 rows.

2 Lay out seven blocks and 18 setting triangles as shown. Sew the pieces into nine diagonal units. Sew the units together to complete row B. Press. Make a total of five B rows.

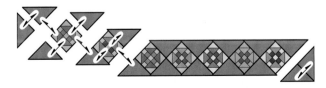

Row B.
Make 5 rows.

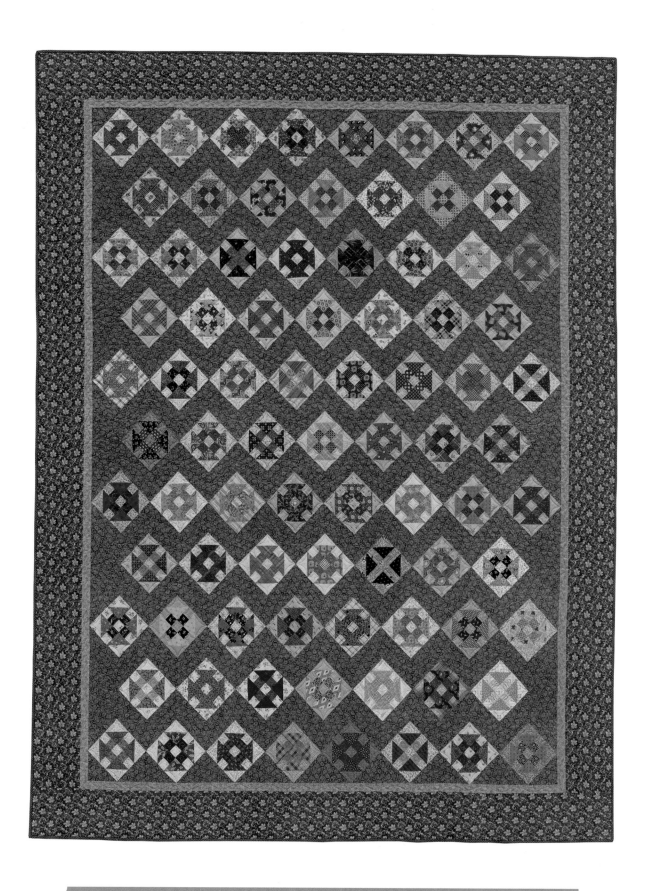

*Give and Take, pieced by **Carol Hopkins** and quilted by **Lisa Ramsey***

3 Sew the A and B rows together, alternating them as shown in the quilt assembly diagram below. Press after adding each row.

4 For the inner border, join seven light gray 1½"-wide strips end to end. Measure the length of the quilt top through the center and cut two light gray strips to this measurement. Sew the strips to the sides of the quilt and press.

5 Measure the width of the quilt top through the center, including the just-added border pieces, and cut two light gray strips to that length. Sew the strips to the top and bottom of the quilt and press.

6 Repeat steps 4 and 5, without sewing the strips together, to add the gray-and-tan print 6"-wide outer-border strips.

7 Layer the quilt top, batting, and backing. Baste the layers together and hand or machine quilt. The quilt shown is machine quilted with swirls and scallops in the blocks, leaves, and vines in the inner border, and feather designs in the setting triangles and outer border.

8 Trim the excess batting and backing. Use the gray dot 2"-wide strips to bind the quilt. Add a hanging sleeve, if desired, and a label.

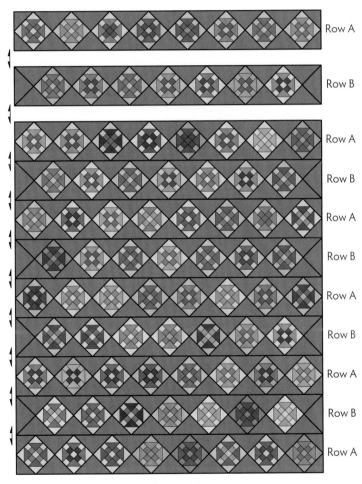

Row A

Row B

Row A

Row B

Row A

Row B

Row A

Row B

Row A

Row B

Row A

Quilt assembly

Tribute to Judie

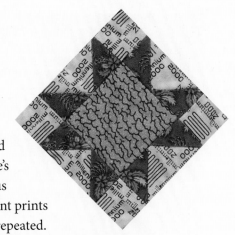

Do you have a quilting idol? Mine is Judie Rothermel, whose reproduction fabrics I've collected since her first line debuted in 1987. I didn't start out with a plan to hoard— I mean "collect"—them, but every time she released new prints, I just had to have them. I had always wanted to make a quilt using as many of Judie's fabrics as possible, and her twentieth anniversary of designing for Marcus Fabrics seemed to be the perfect occasion. This quilt contains 540 different prints used as star points, star centers, and block backgrounds with no fabrics repeated.

FINISHED QUILT: 64" × 76¾" ◆ FINISHED BLOCK: 3" × 3"

Materials

Yardage is based on 42"-wide fabric.

180 assorted light scraps, at least 4" × 6" *each*, for block backgrounds

180 assorted medium scraps, at least 2" × 2" *each*, for star centers

180 assorted dark scraps, at least 3" × 6" *each*, for star points

2 yards of red-and-tan print for setting squares and triangles

2 yards of stripe print for inner and middle borders*

2⅛ yards of red-and-brown print for outer border and binding**

4⅔ yards of fabric for backing

70" × 83" piece of batting

*The quilt shown includes borders cut from different stripes in the same fabric. If you prefer to use two different nondirectional prints, you'll need ¼ yard of a red print for the inner border and ½ yard of a light print for the middle border. You can also cut just one wider border following the cutting note on page 77.

**The yardage listed assumes binding strips are cut on the lengthwise grain. If you prefer to cut your binding crosswise, you'll need 2⅝ yards.

To Add Interest

When selecting fabric for the setting squares and triangles, choose a nondirectional small-scale print that is medium in value. To make your blocks pop, it should be darker than most of the light backgrounds, but not as dark as most of the star points.

Cutting

All measurements include ¼"-wide seam allowances.

From *each* of the light scraps, cut:
4 rectangles, 1¼" × 2" (720 total)
4 squares, 1¼" × 1¼" (720 total)

From *each* of the medium scraps, cut:
1 square, 2" × 2" (180 total)

From *each* of the dark scraps, cut:
8 squares, 1¼" × 1¼" (1,440 total)

From the red-and-tan print, cut:
14 strips, 3½" × 42"; crosscut into 154 squares, 3½" × 3½"
2 strips, 5½" × 42"; crosscut into 13 squares, 5½" × 5½". Cut into quarters diagonally to yield 52 side triangles (2 are extra).
2 squares, 3" × 3"; cut in half diagonally to yield 4 corner triangles

Continued on page 77

75

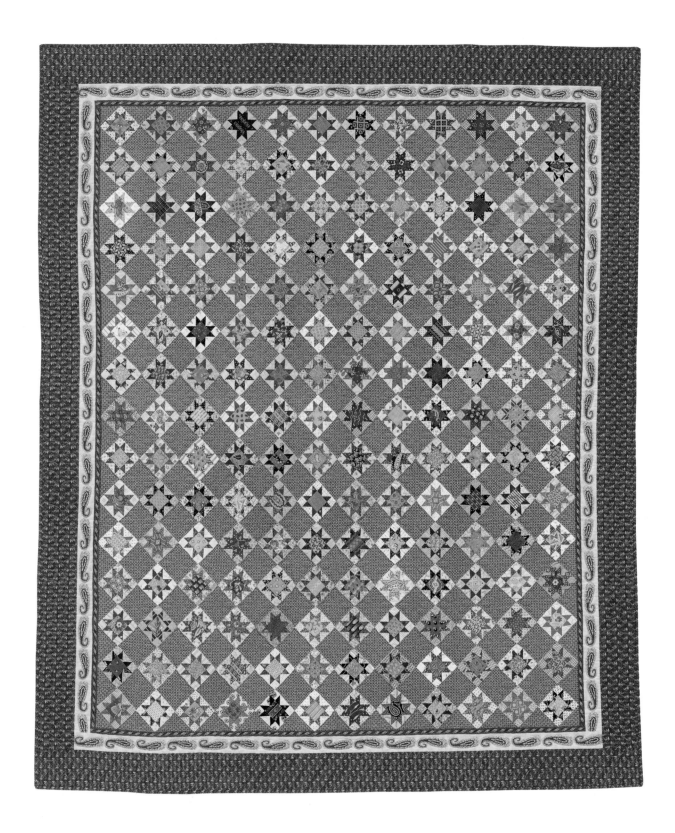

Tribute to Judie, pieced by *Carol Hopkins* and quilted by *Lisa Ramsey*

Continued from page 75

From the *lengthwise* grain of the stripe print, cut: *
4 red strips, 1" × 72"
4 light strips, 2¼" × 72"

From the *lengthwise* grain of the red-and-brown print, cut:
4 strips, 4½" × 74"
4 strips, 2" × 74" (for binding)

*To simplify the border construction you can cut four lengthwise strips measuring 2¾" × 72" rather than separate inner and middle borders. If using nondirectional fabrics for the inner and middle borders, cut 6 red strips, 1" × 42", for the inner border and 6 light strips, 2¼" × 42", for the middle border.

Making the Blocks

Each block contains a light, medium, and dark print. Instructions are for making one block. Press the seam allowances as indicated by the arrows.

1. Draw a diagonal line from corner to corner on the wrong side of eight matching dark 1¼" squares. Place a marked square on one end of a light 1¼" × 2" rectangle with right sides together as shown. Stitch along the drawn line, and then trim the seam allowances to ¼" if desired. Press. Stitch, trim, and press a marked square to the other end of the same rectangle. Make four units measuring 1¼" × 2", including seam allowances.

Make 4 units,
1¼" × 2".

2. Arrange four matching light 1¼" squares, the units from step 1, and a medium 2" square as shown. Sew the pieces together into rows, and then join the rows. Make 180 Star blocks measuring 3½" square, including seam allowances.

Make 180 blocks,
3½" × 3½".

Assembling and Finishing

For more help with any of the finishing steps, you'll find free information at ShopMartingale.com/HowtoQuilt.

1 Arrange the Star blocks and the red-and-tan setting squares in diagonal rows as shown. Add the red-and-tan side and corner triangles.

2 Sew the blocks, setting squares, and side triangles together in diagonal rows and press.

3 Sew the rows together, pressing after adding each row. Add the corner triangles and press.

4 Trim the quilt top if necessary, leaving a ¼" seam allowance beyond the points of the blocks.

5 For the inner border, measure the length of the quilt top through the center and trim two of the red 1"-wide strips to this measurement. Sew the strips to the sides of the quilt and press. If you are using a nondirectional fabric, join the six red 1"-wide strips, end to end, and then cut the lengths you need for the inner side borders. If you have combined the inner and middle borders as one 2¾" strip, use that in place of the red 1"-wide strips and omit the steps for the middle border.

6 Measure the width of the quilt top through the center, including the just-added inner border pieces, and cut two red 1"-wide strips to this measurement. Sew the strips to the top and bottom of the quilt and press.

7 Repeat steps 5 and 6 for the light middle border and the red-and-brown outer border.

8 Layer the quilt top, batting, and backing. Baste the layers together and hand or machine quilt. The quilt shown is machine quilted with a flower design in the setting squares, outline quilting of the paisley motifs in the middle border, and a feather design in the outer border.

9 Trim the excess batting and backing fabric. Use the red-and-brown 2"-wide strips to bind the quilt. Add a hanging sleeve, if desired, and a label.

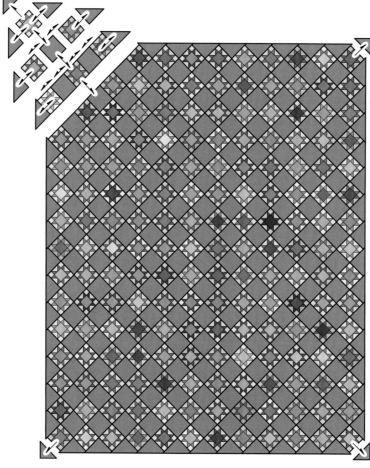

Quilt assembly

ACKNOWLEDGMENTS

While my name is the only name on the cover of this book, there are many people who have contributed to *Vintage Legacies*. I was going to say that you are all amazing, but when I looked up that term in the thesaurus, hoping to find a word that captured how beyond amazing you are, I found all of these words to describe you: astonishing, astounding, remarkable, wonderful, incredible, marvelous, and miraculous.

First, thank you to all of the Martingale editors and staff for sharing your creative and technical skills. I greatly appreciate your attention to the smallest of details as you take computer files, rough line drawings, and a box of quilts and turn them into a beautiful book.

I owe special thanks to Lisa Ramsey for using her magical machine quilting powers to add feathery designs to my pieced quilt tops on the tightest of deadlines. Sue Hellenbrand, Marilyn Poppelwell, and Carol Alberts also shared their special gifts as they completed lovely machine quilting designs on quilts included in this collection.

I've always said I'm going to become good at appliqué in my next life, since that skill doesn't appear to be showing up in this one. Luckily, I'm fortunate to have a talented friend like Pam Schweitzer, who appliquéd the medallion center of the Enduring Love quilt when all I provided were some bird, branch, and leaf shapes and a rough sketch of where to place them.

And, speaking of friends, Garnet Roesel, Pam Antalis, and the late Linda Koenig and Connie Culverhouse deserve to share the credit for the Work Shirts, Game of Graces, Give and Take, and Faded Roses quilts made from our block exchanges. I treasure our years of sharing quilt blocks as well as all that life brings.

Thanks to Pati Violick of Marcus Fabrics and Laura Jaquinto of Windham Fabrics for continuing to provide me with inspiration packaged in a FedEx box each time you generously send me new reproduction fabric collections.

As always, thank you Mom and Dad, Anne and Bill Horgan, for being the loving and encouraging parents you were. Not a day that goes by that I don't miss you.

ABOUT THE AUTHOR

CAROL HOPKINS lives in West Lafayette, Indiana, where she enjoys spending time with her husband, three children, their spouses, and four beautiful grandchildren. This is her sixth publication with Martingale since 2012, following the success of four best sellers in her "Civil War Legacies" series and *The 4" × 5" Quilt Block Anthology: 182 Blocks for Reproduction Fabrics,* coauthored with the late Linda Koenig.

Carol has created more than 100 individual patterns marketed as "Civil War Legacies" and "Vintage Legacies," showcasing eighteenth- and nineteenth-century reproduction prints. Carol's books and patterns are sold worldwide, and many of her designs have been featured in national and international quilt publications. To learn more about Carol and see further examples of her work, visit CarolHopkinsDesigns.com.